THE ESSENTIAL PAIN AND PEACE OF LIFE

Copyright © Jason A. Benefield, 2023
First Edition

ISBN 978-1-914447-80-8 (Hardcover)
ISBN 978-1-914447-81-5 (ebook)

All rights reserved. No part of this book may be reproduced in any form, including photocopying and recording, without permission in writing from the publisher, except for brief quotes in review or reference.

This book details the author's personal experiences and is not a substitute for professional legal or medical advice. The content of this book is for informational purposes only and is not intended to diagnose, treat, cure, or prevent any condition or disease. Please seek advice from your healthcare provider for your personal health concerns prior to taking healthcare advice from this book.

Neither the publisher nor the author is engaged in rendering professional advice or services to the reader. The ideas, suggestions, and procedures provided in this book are not intended as a substitute for seeking professional guidance. Neither the publisher nor the author shall be held liable or responsible for any loss or damage allegedly arising from any suggestion or information contained in this book

Although this book is a work of creative non-fiction based on true events, some names and identifiers, as well as certain events and incidents, have been changed to best suit the narrative and protect those involved.

Book Design by Sean Patrick, TGH: The Good House Ltd.

Prepared by TGH: The Good House Ltd.
www.TGHBooks.com

THE ESSENTIAL PAIN AND PEACE OF LIFE

THE JOURNEY OF UNFOLDING CONSCIOUSNESS

JASON A. BENEFIELD

CONTENTS

Acknowledgments   7
Introduction   11

1. You Are a Commodity   21
2. Resistance is Futile   55
3. Pain Helps Create Your Environment   83
4. Be Honest with Yourself   111
5. The Conscious and Subconscious Minds are Key   133
6. Co-Create the Life You Deserve   163
7. Your Word is Your Bond   179
8. Enjoy Being Who You Are   191
9. You Are a Leader Too   209
10. In Midst of the Hurt Think Positively   225
11. Be You by Being Peace   235

Bibliography   255

ACKNOWLEDGMENTS

There are many to whom I would like to express my gratitude.

First and foremost, I give thanks to God, the Universal Source, the Great One in my life. Thank You for awakening me to your greatness and for the unlimited information and knowledge that You have bestowed upon me.

To my grandparents Sam Benefield Sr., Annie Mae and Robert Lewis, and Joseph and Ethel Peeler, Sr. – Thank you for instilling wisdom and an understanding of God's will in the lives of your children, which has been passed to me. I hold the memory of each of you in my heart and give thanks for the stories and memories that keep you alive.

To my parents Sam and Lalla Benefield Jr. – Thank you for raising me to be a young man who honors the Universal One as his one and only source. Thank you for instilling courage in me, and for giving me my first book to read from a fellow motivational speaker, Les Brown. I'm grateful.

To my Uncle Joe Peeler II – Thank you for being a great pillar in my life and taking the time to teach me the ways of the Great One. Thank you for the infinite wisdom that you shared with me; it helped me to expand and now I get to share this with others. I miss you and you will never be forgotten.

To my Aunt Diane Peeler Ashford – Thank you for being a second mother to me. You talked, laughed, chastised, cooked, and cared for me like I was your child. You are missed and I wish that you could have seen this book before your transition. I will carry your memory in my heart forever.

To my Aunt and Godmother Betty Jean McCarley – "Hey Babe!" I miss hearing this phrase anytime I'd talk on the phone with you. Your excitement and willingness to live life was infectious. I miss your dancing, singing, laughing, playing games, and cooking like grandma. When I dance, I dance for you. Thank you for showing me how to live life without regret.

To My Aunt Lorraine E. Peeler (my Trekkie companion) – Thank you for teaching me to speak with integrity and to teach with authority. You demonstrated for me how to follow my heart (the spirit) to achieve anything that I want. Thank you for being my pastor, teacher, and most importantly, my aunt. "May you live long and prosper, in eternal life."

To My Cousin Paul Garlington – Thank you for showing my uncle Joe the path to Truth Teaching. You as Spirit is the reason, I'm on the path I'm on now. Has become an Agape Licensed Spiritual Practitioner and soon a Reverend. You led me to Rev. Michael and Agape.

To Chris Roland – Thank you for being my mentor in the beginning stages of my journey as a motivational speaker. Your encouragement will always be a foundation for me as I move into greater arenas.

To Kelwin Hagen thank you so much for you time, energy, and expertise on taking my photos for the book cover. Thank you for your yes.

To DeAnna Carpenter you have definitely use the eye beyond the eye as you edited my book. I am so grateful for you yes and how this project became as wonderful as it is. You are simply marvelous.

INTRODUCTION

The idea of Your Quality of Life, now The Essential Pain and Peace of Life, came to me when I was part of a multi-level marketing team. I was a member of the team for six years and during that time, I learned from successful people in the company, and gained knowledge from many different books that I had read. It was rejected by the upline (leader) when I presented it to him and now you have the benefit it today. As I was writing this book, I noticed how my pain just like I experienced from my upline rejecting the program, help shaped my journey into who I am today and that I have learned so much from what I experienced in my life. I also noticed how often little

Introduction

Jason come forth wanting to be soothed of that very pain that he had experienced growing up. Because that energy wasn't properly transmuted, it showed up constantly in his relationships with others and himself. The pain and hurt that I experienced in my life was the true focal point of why I wanted to experience peace as my life. Also, to see the greatness that I am and become more of, that I kept hearing Essence say either to me directly or through other people. I realized talking about my experience with pain is the right direction; this is how I would present my message of helping people transform their pain into purpose.

Growing up with my family, I noticed how talking about the pain and or emotions in general was a taboo. Being a man of African descent in America, I was told that a man doesn't show any weakness of any kind, that includes talking about your emotions, crying, and looking or feeling sad. Everything had to be held in, yet I never learned how to properly deal with pain I had when no one was looking. I experienced that it was same for a large number of families that were also of African descent. Generally, whatever harm that took place would be swept under the rug or buried in the subconscious mind. This project that I'm embarking on was indeed something that wasn't common to even look into because there wouldn't be a space created for people to be listened to for what is coming up for them to be revealed and healed. I have created that space and this space is available to all who wants to come and be a part of it. I'm also breaking the mold so that more people can be healed and free by their pain and not bondage by it, yet they have to let it come forth and be with it in order for the process to work. That is the only way to release what no longer serves the person and body.

Even though I believed to have created this program/book because of my experience with being a part of the multilevel marketing business, to help those in the business to realize that their greatness is and has always been within each of them, to accomplish anything and everything that they desire, was no longer the impetus for this movement. It is truly and totally allowing the hurt and the pain of one's life to actually work for their benefit, to allow it to actually be their friend and manifest the life one truly desires and deserves. I get it, it's totally difficult and unconscionable to comprehend and come to terms with the fact that pain has its place in the process of life unfoldment. That was what I was experiencing in the moment I noticed how much revelation I was receiving based on the search for myself in the midst of the pain and hurt I went

Introduction

through out my life. This was the Star Trek I was on to know my inner being that is my true life.

So, I totally surrendered to this idea and now created The Essential Pain and Peace of Life. Michael Beckwith my spiritual teacher, leader and director of Agape International Spiritual Center stated that, "surrendering is yielding to the next stage of your unfoldment." Indeed, I yielded to the next stage of the unfolding of this book and to the hurt and pain that I have experienced in my life. I made the painful experiences my friends and helpers fully and completely. I didn't see them as being good or bad, yet just is. They were exactly what they were supposed to be in order for me to know and understand who I am as an individualized expression of the very power and presence, Source, Universe, that I call True Essence which is the very power that I tap into to manifest the very life that I have and will continue to unfold moment by moment.

I began my journey in turning, "Your Quality of Life" into "The Essential Pain and Peace of Life" as a public speaking program. This transition took place when I was introduced to Samika Sullivan, a young woman who was very diligent in working with the youth and was a director of a program in Niagara Falls, New York. The main purpose of the meeting at the time was for her to join my team in the multi-level marketing business. Yet there was something else brewing that would turn my life around. After meeting with Samika, she asked me to come to Niagara Falls and speak to the youth at a seminar that she coordinated every year. I was so thrilled that I began rewriting the proposal that I initially pitched for my upline. I wrote a speech that would be suitable for the youth. It turned out that it was something that everyone could grasp and relate to. I understood that everyone needed to understand that from pain to peace was an essential in life, that freedom wasn't for someone else to give them, and that it was crucial for the youth to understand the importance of their self-worth and greatness. This speech was a spark that ignited my passion to help others and served as the foundation for this book.

This journey that I am on has allowed me to realize my self-worth and has taught me that I'm constantly unfolding. Unfoldment is a continual process. It never stops as there is always something greater that wants to show itself through me. This process allows not only things that I want to accomplish to happen yet makes me available to other opportunities and areas of growth and expansion. I'm reminded of a passage I read in the book, "The Man Who Tapped the Secrets of the Universe," by Glenn Clark, which talks about the great transcendent

Introduction

master, universalist, and mystic, Russel Wilson. Wilson was able to accomplish many things without having any prior knowledge on how to do it. From painting a family portrait to sculpting faces to manifesting money when he didn't have sufficient funds to much more, Wilson didn't bind himself to one way of thinking or experiencing life. For him, it was second nature to be open and available to anything he put his mind to. And he did it with great ease because he said yes and allowed it to happen.

I could relate to having ideas and dreams and knowing that it was possible for me to achieve them. For me, the confusing part was that I was told multiple times that I was important and going to do wonderful things with my life, yet I didn't know that to be true for myself. I didn't believe I could do the wonderful things that I or someone else saw me doing with my life. For some reason, I thought I would feel excited hearing someone else tell me about who I was and should be, and what I could accomplish. I later discovered that only I could do this work of knowing my value, worth, and what I would contribute.

When I first created this book and program, I did it because I wanted to prove to others that I was someone of importance and I could be whatever I wanted and said I could be. After learning and understanding what life has to show and teach me especially through the pain experience in my life, I found out that I didn't need to prove anything to anyone. I just had to know my self-worth. I had to prove to myself who I AM, how my life should unfold, and what was important to and about me. If my goal was to help others also understand who they are for themselves, then I had to do this work for myself first.

It is important to me that whatever I do, I do it with joy and peace. I have discovered through my journey that I am peace itself. It's because I embraced the paid that I experienced in my life and made it my ally to see what is needed to be released and let freedom ring as my life. With that understanding, I'm able to accomplish whatever it is that I want. Inner Peace is experienced when we allow life to unfold and our true nature to express itself. There is a feeling of accomplishment even before the manifestation has been revealed. This means that no matter what state I'm in physically, there should be a feeling of peace that prepares the mind to receive the idea and dreams in whichever form they manifest. This is through acknowledging the pain that I have allowed to hinder me from seeing, moving with courage, ease and grace, to my greatest life that has been prepared from me by Essence. I am learning to create more and joy and peace and as I do, I realize my oneness with True Essence, the God presence within.

Introduction

When I began to apply the principles and concepts discussed in this book, I opened myself to a new way of learning and understanding that allowed me to focus on my quality of life through my pain and hurt. I have also learned a myriad of ways to accomplish my visions and acquire what I need to achieve them. I began developing a stronger relationship with Essence and I began the journey of releasing everything that (and everyone who) no longer had a place in my life. Everything I focused on became possible. There were no limitations, only the ones that I set for myself.

You have this same power within you. There is something inside of you that wants to come out and propel you into the greatest rendition of your life. Everything about the Spirit within you is essential for growth and it already possesses the awareness of what you are destined to become. It is vitally important that it comes forth and is manifest in your life. You have to know that you're worthy of only the greatest that True Essence has to offer, no matter what you are going through.

In this book, I share my journey to awakening to and embracing the essential pain and peace of life. I go into detail tips and insights that I've learned on my spiritual journey on how hurt and pain has assisted me in opening to more of the greatness that True

Essence already knew and had in store for me. I also share, through personal anecdotes and story, how I overcame my challenge of seeking approval and validation from others. And I share intimately about the painful and hurtful struggles I moved through to unfold into a greater version of me. It is my hope that you hear yourself in the words on these pages and that you're encouraged to continue to surrender to the pain, to be peace, which is not only essential to life, yet also your true nature.

A quick disclaimer, you will notice that I use a lot of scripture from the Bible. I was raised to read and believe in the bible, yet I use that scriptures that have affirmative meaning to life and help to give dynamic to the information that I provide in this book. I'm not religious, I'm Spiritual.

Are you ready! Let's Go!

1
YOU ARE A COMMODITY

Commodity – n. Something or someone that is useful or valued.
~ Merriam-Webster Dictionary

When a person hears the word commodity, the first thought, I believe, would be like the definition above and would include things such as an article of trade, commerce, goods, and metals. These things have been given value and have been determined by someone to have value. A lot of emphasis and significance has been placed on material possessions being a commodity, and very little attention has been placed on the greatest commodity of them all – human beings. A living, co-creating, life-expressing being. Just think about it: This human incarnation is given to us free of charge, to be lived and expressed to the fullest, complete with greatness, talents, dreams, and ideas that was infused in us since our conception on this planet. This body, which was created and formed to house the very Spirit that created us, can walk, talk, take care of itself, dream the biggest dreams, execute those dreams with joy, control vehicles, and much more. Have you ever wondered why human life isn't at the top of the list as being the most valuable entity on this planet?

There is a disconnect. When a person – despite his/her color, creed, sexual orientation, religious and financial status – has determined the value of how another person should be revered. Unfortunately, this way of being, or judgment, is what I believe was taught to us. We have been taught to give value to things more than the people who help us acquire those very material possessions – the very people who named and brought meaning to the very things that are held to be more useful and valuable than the person(s) who created it. This, to me, is limiting and doesn't allow the full spectrum of life to be shown and noticed. As people, we were created to be great thinkers, creators, and the like, and have been given something that is greater than any article of trade, commerce, goods, and metals. We have been given the right (and power) to make something with those very things and create a lot of the material possessions that we are enjoying today. With the power source of Spirit, you *are* the commodity, and you are to know that for yourself. You are to live day by day with the understanding that you aren't here by mistake. You were created to do wonderful and marvelous things and to be a benefit to people on this planet.

COMMODITY CONSCIOUSNESS

Growing up I didn't have the best time knowing and understanding my value and importance here on earth. Having an illness that I didn't know about or had any control over, lead me to believing what others thought and believed about me. The hurt and pain that I endured by my parents because of the illness led me to believe that I wasn't worthy of being here and that I had to prove myself and my value. I realized that I was driven by pain to try to fix something that wasn't even really broken. I didn't know any better at that time and continued to have people outside of myself to establish my value and importance for my life. I put my trust in another human, which failed because it wasn't in alignment to what and who I am created to be. It was much later when I had co-created this idea of Commodity Consciousness that assisted me in reminding myself who and who's I am, that helped make a difference in my life and allow me to know, see, and reveal through my creativity my true value and importance on this planet. In what area of your life that hurt and pain has allowed you to believe that you aren't useful or valuable?

When this idea of knowing that you are useful and of value fully settles in, you won't have the time to worry about what other people say about you. You will begin to walk taller knowing that whatever idea, dream, and goal that is brought to your awareness, is what is given to you to do and give to the world, because you are the chosen one. That's right: You are the chosen one. You are Neo in this life. You have a calling to set forth anything and everything that is coming to mind that will help uplift other people on this Earth to be their greatest selves. You are the very light that is going to shine and direct millions of souls to express the very essence of who they really are, which is joy, love, peace, harmony, and overall productive. This is what you are created to be and do. However, and wherever you see yourself being a benefit and expressing your value in the world, please do so with your whole wonderful and loving heart.

Your awareness that you are of value and importance is paramount to your total existence on this Earth. This is not about being noticed, getting permission, or seeking validation from anyone. This is about your own self-worth and loving yourself so much that you get to enjoy living this life that Essence has made. You get to rejoice and be glad that you are here to make the greatest contribution known to you and expressed to all. This is what I know to be true and why I believe having a Commodity Consciousness is crucial in everyday living. With commodity consciousness you get to be your full self without compromise, withhold, or worry because you know that you are worth it. You are worth it because you are valuable and important. That is all that matters.

I feel it is the truth of all of us, no matter what one's current situation or status is, that we are useful and are of value to Life itself. Since there are things *given* value and importance without any argument, what if that same value or more is given to one who is connected with a power and presence that lives as and through them? This is why it's important to know and understand you are one of importance and value: You are fully fueled, filled, and made of the very Spirit that lives in everything. I believe that people are created to truly show and express the very essence that is creative, loving, compassionate, and abundant and because a person is created to reveal that very expression, that is what makes them valuable and important. A person is created to show the very ideas, dreams, and goals that is calling within them to co-create. Since this is true for everyone, then it's time to know who you really are. It's time to walk heavy on this Earth, leaving nothing yet a trail of the wonderful and marvelous outcomes from the very creative ideas, dreams, and goals revealed from within.

The value and importance of a person is worth more than any materials that can be traded or any form of commerce. It doesn't make sense to me how a person can harm another and devalue that person's life yet fully embrace a material possession that can't even relate or connect to them on a soul-to-soul level. There's a belief planted over time that having a nice home in a specific area, the money to purchase it, prestige, clothing, and social status means "what I have makes me better than you." I know this because I have not only done this, yet I believed it and tried to live from this. I grew up around nice things, lived in nice homes, and didn't want for much. I have experienced my mother and father openly communicate to me at different times how the house and car had more value than I. Now, that is how I felt at the time of the communication, yet it didn't make me feel like I was worth more to them then the material possessions at the time. I remember having a conversation with an acquaintance and at the time, she was enraged by something I had said. I told her that I was better than her because the home my parents purchased was newly built and her house wasn't. I remember the sadness in her eyes because she was hurt that a fellow Hue-man (black person) would say something like, especially one (me) who wanted all Hue-mans in the area to stick together and have a common bond (we lived in a predominately white area that had its unique differences). At that time, I didn't know and realize that me and my acquaintance were far greater than where we lived and our possessions. I was passing to my acquaintance the very pain I experienced from my parents to her, as a way to transmute my energy from feeling unvalued to valued. Our beingness and who we are is greater than any material thing that is created. The value of the things we create does not, and will never, supersede the value of the life that we are living right now.

We are created to be, do, create, and have things beyond the human imagination. Because of this, it's imperative that every idea, dream, and goal be heard, cultivated, nurtured, and expressed. This expression is the birthright of every person. We each are gifted with these ideas, dreams, and goals to show the glory of the power within. Yes you, a person of value and importance, are made in the image and likeness of the Essence within. The moment I gave myself permission to believe that I am valuable and important because of that which is within me, everything shifted. I acknowledged the pain of being less than, unworthy, unvaluable and made a shift in my belief and thinking about myself, that I am greater thank, worthy and valuable. I did this for me. The belief I instilled is unmistakable, undisputable, and unchangeable. I gave **myself** the value that is rightfully mine to identify myself as valuable and important, and I didn't wait for anyone to confirm or validate my value. I carried that belief so it would be felt, known, and realized by others. I am a commodity and I believe this to be true for everyone. It's self-generated and starts with our belief in ourselves first. You are a commodity. Own it, believe it, and receive it.

WEEDING OUT THE PAIN OF THE BS (BELIEF SYSTEM)

ADMITTEDLY, IT TOOK SOME TIME FOR ME TO EMBRACE the truth that I am valuable and important. For the longest time – since I was about 8 years old – I believed that I was anything yet valuable and important. After I had my seizure (or black out as my mother called it) during service at my family church, I woke up in the lower level of the church to a conversation between my mother and a fellow church member who was a nurse. What I heard from the person that I believed loved me, couldn't do no wrong, and could only see productivity in me, rocked my belief for a long period of time in my life. Caused a lot of pain my life and trust in what other women may believe about me and I about myself. I heard the nurse say, "You need to take him to the hospital and see a doctor." My mother replied, "There is nothing wrong with him, he is just being bad." I was dazed from the experience and clueless to what happened to me, yet what I remembered and continued to remember from that moment was what my mother said. I was crushed because I never wanted to be seen as a bad child in my mothers' eyes. From that moment on, I committed to receiving external validation from other people to be known as someone of value and importance. It was that moment I became a people pleaser and allowed my light to be diminished for the sake of being what I believed to be acceptable and aesthetic to those around me.

My confidence was dormant, and I didn't have faith in my ability to make decisions. As a result, I began to ask others what they thought was best for me. Anytime that I felt or thought someone saw me as a bad person, I took it as my duty to make their perception of me great and unforgettable in the most positive way possible, even if the person never thought I was bad. I didn't know that I was someone of value and importance, because I held on to the belief that I was a bad boy. I then added the belief that no one would want to love or be around me. What I didn't realize was that I was making myself invaluable and unimportant to myself first and foremost, not to anyone else. Now that I am aware of this belief and where it began, I can now love it, release it, and replace it with the undisputed truth that I am someone of value and importance. I matter. I was created to do wonderful and marvelous things with this life.

OF VALUE & IMPORTANCE

ACCEPTING AND INTERNALIZING THAT YOU ARE A Commodity is essential to knowing your true nature as Peace, regardless of what someone else may think they know about you or more importantly, what you say about yourself that doesn't vibe with the Truth of who you are. You are someone of value and importance. Before we go further, let's look at what value and importance mean.

Value is something that has been given worth, usually to material things, by someone. The dictionary states it as, "the monetary worth of something, relative worth or importance." I believe this definition can be applied to people, especially when they take the time to know and understand they are of value. And value isn't something that is bestowed upon you by someone in a certain position. You are the authority, and you are in the divine right position to know your value because of that which created you, the Essence within. You do not have to wait again for someone to give you what you already are. You already possess the value within you. You already have what it takes to be more than your current situation. Everything is working for your good. Your value is measured by the very power and presence that is within and has been there since the beginning of time. Once you tune in to Essence, you can begin to energize yourself and manifest a life in the way that it's intended to be because you are someone of value. You were created to be of value.

Being ill wasn't anything that I had control over, yet it was looked at as a way of being disrespectful and a bad child. Deep down I knew that I had value, yet I couldn't get over the story that was imprinted on my mind. I had continued the story with my own ideas and didn't see myself as valuable. It even got to the point where others noticed the story and added to it. That was a challenge, because I always knew that I was created for greatness, yet I put my own obstacles in the way of me living a full life of value.

Eventually, I learned to stand tall in what I knew for myself. It took time for me to change my story from non-valuable to someone that is of value. I knew that when I began to change my mind it was going to become a journey of a lifetime. I faced what wasn't true about me and began to speak the Truth, "I'm someone of value" daily. I even created boundaries for myself and envisioned that I was the master of my immediate bubble, mind, and soul.

I acknowledged my value and believed it so much that others noticed it. Granted, there were some people who didn't like the change because they were used to the old me. They served as mirrors, reflecting to me the old beliefs I held of myself and presented me with the opportunity to face it and speak the truth of my identity. With this practice, I didn't wait for someone else to establish or validate my value, yet they noticed my value anyway and simply acknowledged it. It's time for you to believe and know that you are of value so much so that it exudes out of your pores daily.

IMPORTANCE

WHEN CONTINUING TO UNDERSTAND THE TRUE NATURE of yourself on this planet and how you present through your dreams, ideas, and goals, we go to the second part of the definition of Commodity which is indicative with knowing that you are already important. I believe that you were automatically created to be someone of importance, as the expression of True Essence. The definition of important is, "of much or great significance. Mattering much. Entitled to more than ordinary consideration or notice. Prominent. Of considerable influence or authority." These qualities are also something that is already within each of us and have been ingrained in the DNA of every person. I know this to be true for myself and I also know this to be true for you.

With the practice of constant awareness, you will begin to feel the Peace that you are. That's why acknowledging the pain you feel is intricate to revealing your worth and opening yourself to a greater way of being. When the pain arises, there is a moment where you will begin to see where, what, and who, needs to be released for the healing to begin. Worry, doubt, low self-esteem, and disbelief in yourself will begin to dissolve, all because you are focusing on your truth. My goal in this chapter and book is to begin to forge a new frontier in your mind. To help you open and allow yourself to know and see yourself differently – all from the perspective of your true nature as a person of peace, value, and importance.

MY JOURNEY TO COMMODITY CONSCIOUSNESS

As I reached my late teens, I noticed that people felt that my numerous skill sets came in handy in different capacities of life and areas of business. Even though I was still functioning with the pain and hurt that I buried inside from my past experience, to try to show that I can be of some valuable to others. I was still finding my way through the illusions of the beliefs I created about myself. Yet, the skills, talents, and abilities were growing and showing forth and that is something that be determined when and where they will appear. As I started to discover my purpose in life, I began to develop these innate abilities such as my courage to talk to people I didn't know, the ability to speak and sing in front of large crowds, and my attention to detail when planning an event or recalling valuable information to secure a deal or a sale, to name just a few. These abilities are my commodities, which are of great value to others and to myself. There were people who noticed that I am a commodity and they saw potential I didn't know I had. My value and importance were not only noticed, yet they were also matched by other great minds. This miraculous conception took place because I was open to being a commodity and allowed myself to express as I am.

In my journey of unfolding, I practiced changing my mindset to be an open and willing vessel to serve. I understood a long time ago that I was chosen to do remarkable things. To better understand what I was to do, I would sit in the silence and receive information from the Source within to co-create my ideas and dreams. I made the choice to become a leader and lead individuals in unfolding continuously into their greatness. I chose to be someone who helps others reveal and understand who they were already destined to be since before they were born. I know that being the true self is much better than being what someone else thinks is best for a person to be.

When I was a young child, my cousins, siblings, and I would play church. Each time we play I would always be the guest speaker and my cousin Joe would be the host pastor. He would introduce me to our play congregation, and we would greet each other with a hug and handshake, just like we saw our predecessors do growing up in the church. As I was giving the message, they would encourage me to get loud and excited, just to get them excited. They would begin to worship, shout, and dance. We thought it was all fun and games until I turned 16. That's when I realized I could be a voice who would speak to the masses, yet at that time I had no one to help me develop. After two speaking engagements, I put those dreams aside because I didn't know who I could turn to and how to become the speaker I was meant to be. Plus, I was young, and I didn't know what I wanted to do with my life at the time, even though that feeling to speak was always there. Years later, I moved away from home to various cities and states in hope of starting a life that I thought was for me. No matter where I went something would go wrong and I would find myself right back in Buffalo, New York.

This back and forth happened three times in 11 years. When I returned, I went back to my home church, Covenant Truth Center, and worked with my Aunt Lorraine, my mother's sister. A few months after, I became the Praise and Worship leader, a minister, and began to develop my prophetic gift. I didn't want such a responsibility better yet; I didn't know how to handle the responsibility given. Subconsciously I was still holding on to the pain and belief that I'm not a productive person and I cannot do what I was appointed to do. My aunt saw something inside me that needed to come out and to be used for Divine's glory. My Uncle Joe, my mother's brother, gave me books and extra teaching that assisted me on my path. Things turned around for me because I finally embraced my inner dreams. I allowed the continuation of the modification process to work on my behalf to become the entity that I am today. When I wasn't focused on fulfilling my abilities, I was unbalanced and running amuck. Once I turned my focus back onto the Source within, I locked into the opportunities that where being prepared for me. The doors began to open for me, and they continue to open.

There were numerous ideas and dreams that I wanted to learn more about, things I thought I wouldn't be able to do because I didn't have the right information, knowledge, and training. I knew that it wasn't enough to just have the ideas and dreams; I also needed to know how to properly execute them. Having locked onto True Essence, another opportunity presented itself to me. Since the age of 20, I wanted to write, play, perform my own songs and open a music production company. I had so many lyrics and melodies going through my head, and I didn't know how to play an instrument, except my voice, or read and write sheet music. I didn't know what it took to make them completed works. I thought it would be a productive idea to hook up with a high school choir, R&B artists, and groups. I hoped to get them to sing my songs, yet they were not interested. I tried working with others that had a vision of being in the music industry and that fell through also. My passion to fulfill my dreams and ideas was very strong and I craved the direction and guidance that it would take to be successful. I continued writing and creating melodies and locked them away hoping to work on them again someday.

After ten years of locking my dreams away in storage, I met Dr. Carol Price and Minister Vernon Chappell who were associates of my Aunt Lorraine.

The Essential Pain and Peace of Life

They talked to me about what True Essence had in store for me and they advised me on what I needed to do to get back on the same frequency of the Universe and manifest the ideas and dreams that I always had. They urged me to read books on songwriting, to get back into the grove of writing new songs and learn what it takes to create better melodies. Two months later, I began to do what these two great individuals advised – I went to Barnes & Nobles and purchased my first book on songwriting. It had everything I needed to know about the different types of melodies, chords that could be created to write great songs, and how to protect them.

    I was taking the initiative to modify my mind to learn music; I wasn't expecting what was going to take place in my life that would catapult me to another level in my learning and in becoming a Commodity. I crossed paths with Mr. Carmen Aquillo, a college professor I hadn't seen in eight years when I went to Erie Community College and took his music theory class. Reuniting with Carmen was the work of the Universe. When I got off work from the printing factory, something inside told me to go to Rite Aid across town to get a Power Aid. As I approached the front of the store to pay for my drink, I heard someone ask me if the store had an ATM. I recognized that it was Mr. Aquillo right away, yet he didn't remember who I was. I reminded him that I was a former student in his Music Theory class. As he thought about it for a moment, he stated that he liked my singing voice when we did classroom exercises. He proceeded to tell me about a music industry program that he taught at Villa Maria, a private college in Buffalo, which he thought I would be great for. Finally, an opportunity had presented itself where I might fulfill my dream of being a creator and producer of music. I went on-line to the college website, to find out what I needed to do to get involved with the music program. I enrolled in the program the very next semester and at last, learned piano, reading and writing sheet music, the ins and outs of business (how to create one and what was needed to start it), how to be a music producer, and took vocal lessons. This was all the result of conversations I had with three influential people who each helped me get back on track. Now I have a Music Industry degree and something I love to do that lets me continue to create music.

The point I'm attempting to make with these stories is that the whole time I was moving in the direction from what I heard from within. I was obedient to receive what rightfully belonged to me. I realized that I am the Commodity and always was. That is what the Universe had prepared me for, even though I took a few detours I was able to get to learn some very productive skills. I believe that there is a voice on the inside that speaks to everyone, no matter who they are and what they do. There were a lot of times that I didn't listen and as I previously mentioned I took some detours. Even though I took those detours I learned a lot along the way of getting back aligned to my true nature. I wouldn't give that knowledge back because it helped me write more songs and perfect playing the piano.

Meeting Samika also showed me how much of a commodity I am. (I mentioned her and how we met in the introduction.) Samika wasn't interested in joining the multi-level marketing team that I was part of. The information I prepared for my multi-level marketing team members, turned out to be the very information that would help change 100s of young people's lives. Samika produced programs for inner-city youth and is one of the directors for a nonprofit arts organization in Niagara Falls, New York. There was something that she saw in me from that day we met, and she knew that I could be a big help to her cause for the youth. Samika told me about an event that she was giving for inner city youth, something she had been doing for many years, and she asked if I would speak at the event. She had absolutely no intention of being a part of the company I was a part of, yet she saw how my enthusiasm and energy would be infectious to others and she valued the information I had to share. My excitement grew about the program. I was finally going to present *The Essential Peace of Life*, the message I thought I created for my marketing team. In August 2005, I presented *The Essential Peace of Life* for the first time in front of over 200 youth and adults. My message was well-received and since that monumental moment, I have been asked to come back several times after.

Knowing that I am a Commodity allowed me to be aware of the seeds within me that had to be cultivated and watered, so the outcome could be blossom into fruition. My gifts were always there for me to see; in some cases, it took someone else to see them and to help me cultivate them to grow into something special. *What seeds do you have within that you haven't allowed to be cultivated?* I implore you to believe that whatever dreams and ideas you desire can happen for you. You are important, you are of value, your seeds are important, and someone is available to help you cultivate them. Those people may be someone you met or acquaintances of family and friends who can see value in what is trying to be brought forth.

EXPLORING COMMODITY CONSCIOUSNESS

When the idea came to me to tell people that they are a commodity, it didn't sit well with me. I resisted in part because the definition mostly attriyeted to the word, and I wasn't sure that others would receive it if they focused on the word without knowing its true definition. I am big on knowing the true definition of a word, an attriyete I got from my Aunt Lorraine. When she preached, she would give the dictionary definition to certain words so that people could understand the context and why she chose those words. For instance, the word rapture as used in the Christian community refers to the end of days, according to the book of Revelations in the Bible. However, when you look up the word in the dictionary, rapture means joy. I prefer to reference the true meaning of the word, just like Anita Baker's song *Rapture*. It sounds and feels better to the soul and provides a more uplifting meaning.

The word commodity is strong, high, and mighty. When you say you are a commodity, you are saying that you are strong in your belief of self, high in the value of your abilities, and mighty in the stature of the great manifestations of your ideas and dreams. I have broken commodity into three parts to further emphasize this. These three parts allowed me to become continuously conscious of being a commodity:

- **Com** (a prefix meaning "with," "together," "in association," and (with intensive force) = ***Communicate***
- **Mod** (root word meaning an act or instance of modifying; modification) = ***Modify***
- **Ity** (a suffix used to form abstract nouns expressing state or condition) = ***Embody***

Com is a prefix that means "together" or "in association." Here is where you connect with Essence through communication. This association is extremely important to recognize, become acquainted with, and have a deep love affair with. The relationship that is being cultivated here is with the self; you are developing an understanding that you are already one with the very life that breathes, lives, moves, and has it's beingness as the very life that is within all people. The human form that houses this life force is in constant connection in the form of communication. Communication is very important because this is where the information is transmitted to reveal the ways and give direction on how to unfold the goals, ideas, and dreams that flow through the mind. Communication comes in different forms including meditation, life visioning, prayer, reading uplifting and high-vibrational literature, and soul-centering music.

To *communicate* means to impart knowledge, transmit, to give or interchange thoughts or information. I have found that communicating to True Essence within is listening to the directions that are being given to me to attain dreams and ideas that are specific to me. Also, through communication I get to see in my visions how to co-create the ideas and dreams by surrendering to the process and allow my steps to be guided by Spirit to bring them into fruition.

Mod, which is the root word means an act or instance of modifying or modification. After communicating with Source and receiving direction, now it's time to **modify** from a state of inactivity to one of activity in creating that true destiny in being a commodity. Modify means, "to change the form or qualities of something; to alter partially." This is where I took on a more productive way of thinking about myself and how I lived my life. I assessed where I was going and what no longer served me in forms of beliefs and ideas, that I acquired from my painful experiences, then performed the necessary practices to begin the modification process. I transformed from being a person living a mediocre life without balance, working a job just to survive, and not allowing myself to be inspired to live fully without worry of mistakes and naysayers to a person who is willing to reveal the hurts of my past and move through the healing process. I had to be the change I wanted to see in my life, which allowed me to create different beliefs and behaviors that freed me from the bondage of what once was.

I had to change the way I thought about obtaining my ideas and dreams. I realized I couldn't continue to think and be like someone who believed they are stuck. I had to rid myself of the negative and toxic ways and mindset, most of which had been passed to me by people who believed they meant well with their advice. I placed all those beliefs and ways of being on the table and examined what I believed as true to the Real Truth. I began the process of breaking free from the mentality that I wasn't productive enough to accomplish anything, I wouldn't have the money, I didn't have the know-how, no one would like anything that I did, and that I could only live and do things within a small box. These beliefs were programmed in my life and had a hold on me, yet I had greater ideas for myself – to be a professional speaker, music producer, author, to be married with children, a beautiful home, multiple acres of land, and travel to extravagant beaches and countries.

I began moving in confidence to obtain the knowledge to unfold my dreams and ideas. I took on personal development in the form of reading books on how to become better with my thoughts. I learned how to honor the feelings that were fighting from being released to understanding myself as a spiritual being. I began to understand money, how to better take care of it and let it work for me, how to be a business owner, and more. This was the new mindset that I needed to be what I knew I could be and more. I was open to being available to meet people who could be beneficial to me in the journey of my unfoldment. I also opened myself to learning on different subjects that would ensure I was successful in the multiple fields I wanted to venture in. I wanted to be in the know and open to more ideas than I could ever imagine.

Modifying myself allowed me to replace unproductive thoughts and beliefs with positive and fulfilling ones by confronting them and feeling what I really wanted in my life, exchanging formerly destructive tendencies with constructive ones. (Like meditation or any form of communication, changing my mindset takes practice.) Also, allowing the pain to assist me in being more aware of what I believed held me back was very essential. Modifying is where the transformation process began. I knew I had to believe in myself and my ideas and dreams before anyone would believe in me. They had to be real and tangible to me before anyone one else could see it. I began to surround myself with people who thought the same way I did and were obtaining their dreams and ideas.

Ity is a suffix used to form abstract nouns expressing state or condition in the process of being. This last part of the process of being a commodity would be to embody everything that I had learned and practiced and make it my way of life from that moment on. **Embody** means, "to give a concrete form to; express, personify, or exemplify in concrete form." This part indeed is a practice as well because there will be moments of forgetting my true nature and what is my new belief system. The more I practice the better I become. The better I become, the more what I know to be true about my life becomes second nature. I continue to unfold, expand, and live fully what I know to be true for my life because I'm living from what is possible and will be done with the backing from True Essence living as my life.

I want you to know that you are real, and you exist on this Earth to do wondrous things in your life right now. You start the process of unfolding into the real you by communing with True Essence, transforming your way of thinking and what you believe about yourself and life, taking the necessary steps in developing how to successfully execute your idea or dream, and becoming more aware of what you're unfolding to be. That is an individual who is useful, who can create and help others become equally as creative and useful, and as the Rev. Dr. Michael Bernard Beckwith, spiritual thought leader and founder of the Agape International Spiritual Center, would say, "A beneficial presence on the planet."

This is a key point to understand: You will now be in a stage of unfolding to be exactly who you are destined to be since the beginning of your time instead of identifying yourself as someone else says you should be. This is the moment where what is important to Essence is important to you. With daily practice of the Commodity Consciousness, you will begin to see so much more that can be accomplished and magnificent levels of unfoldment that can occur. The three parts of becoming a commodity are: **Communication**, where time is taken to listen to the ideas and dreams that are meant to enhance your life; **Modify**, where you begin the process of changing your mindset, by allowing the pain of the past assist in what's to be let go of and learning what it takes to manifest the ideas and dreams; and **Embody**, which is where communicating with Source and modifying life comes together in you becoming who you are meant to be. Taking these steps allow you to become more aware of the peace that is your life, letting the pain of the past dissolve, becoming the change that you would want to be in life and manifesting the ideas and dreams that are available to be accomplished now.

THE COMMODITY SEEDS THAT ARE WITHIN

I CANNOT STRESS THIS ENOUGH: YOU ARE A COMMODITY. You are the highest brand there is. I believe that you should take what you love to do and make it everything to you. Creating businesses, being self-employed, writing books, making music people will enjoy or excelling on your job. You don't have to tell anyone about it, just be affluent. The people you meet will know that you're worth investing in and will join in the cultivating process to create what you love to do.

It's time to be open and ready to receive your rightful inheritance. It's not just one person who is going to take you all the way, though. It's almost like Charles Dickens' book, *A Christmas Carole*, where Ebenezer Scrooge was introduced to three ghosts to help him understand what life was all about and what he could do to not only be a better person, yet to also increase his worth in a positive way. So, it is with you. It may be more than just three people, yet you're open to who comes to add to your potential. They will be people who can help you get closer to understanding what is needed to help manifest a great outcome.

I believe that there are gifts that you have that may not have been tapped into yet, and now is the time to shift your attention to feel and then release any obstacles or fears that may arise when you're attempting to become your true self. Jack Ensign Addington, the author of *Psychogenesis: Everything Begins in Mind*, declares that it's "not a matter of finding yourself, yet of uncovering the true self that is already there. We are really trying to uncover the perfect, divine self that is right here, right within each one of us. It's just as though we were uncovering buried treasure. We must get rid of the debris of negative thinking, the pile of fear thoughts we have entertained over the years, thoughts that have obscured the true self."

Isn't that wonderful? You have the power to uncover your truth by taking the time to feel and love what is not working for you then allow it to dissolve. You have the power to open to hearing what Essence has in store for you to produce unlimited manifestations in your life right now. When you take the time to Love yourself through anything and everything, you will begin to create a new way of experiencing how you will live and create from that moment. Just think about it: Everything within you is suitable for you to succeed. I get extremely excited just thinking about what all is possible and more, a never-ending array of wonderful and magnificent manifestations that will occur no matter what. I'm reminded of lyrics to a song called, "Come Back Home" written by my cousins Larry Garlington and Adel Jones. A verse of the song states: *Becoming what you already are.*

Returning to a place you never left.
Obtaining what you never lost.
Come back home.
Come back home.
Feel the joy; you're a thousand pounds lighter.
See the light; it's a thousand times brighter.
Celebrate, for the answer is within you.
Come back home. Come back home.

WHERE IS HOME? HOME IS ESSENCE THAT IS WITHIN you right now. It is the self that is who you are. Home is everything you possess – the strength, fortitude, abilities, know-how, and most importantly, the very things that can come forth from you via dreams, ideas, and visions. Home is your true self. Believe it or not, because you possess Source power, everything that you see is available and attainable right now!

READY TO UNFOLD?

I BELIEVE KNOWING YOU'RE SOMEONE OF VALUE AND importance is the first essential step to being open to Peace expressing as your life. Feeling through the pain assist in a way that opens you to be aware of what could be hindering you from fully accepting that truth and allow you to manifest life as your true nature. It is a personal journey and shouldn't be taken lightly. When fear of the unknown surfaces, it is because something wonderful and magnificent is ready to come forth as you right now. These are some questions that I think you should ask yourself:

How many times has someone come to me and said they know I can do more?

How many times did I reject the words that were

giving me direction on what can enhance my life and get me closer to my dreams and fulfilling my ideas?

Why am I resisting?

The next chapter will help you understand why fear or resistance is unimportant and to unfold because of and despite it.

2

RESISTANCE IS FUTILE

~

One of my favorite television shows is *Star Trek: The Next Generation*. Its presentation of how distinct species of cultures interacted with each other opened my mind to innovative ideas and gave me a new perspective to approaching life situations to some extent. A recurring menace to the galaxy was a group of beings called the Borg, who were part human and part machine. The Borg swept through space, conquered multiple planets, changed how other civilizations lived, and integrated them into their way of life. The Borg absorbed the whole essence of these other planetary populations, effectively negating the original culture during the assimilation process.

Whenever they encountered a new species, the Borg would declare "Resistance is futile. You will be assimilated!"

Unlike the Borgs, I'm not here to force you to become something that you're not; I am here to help you understand and unfold to what and who you already are. The assimilation I am committed to and speak of is nothing more than you awakening to the true being that is within and allowing that to unfold moment by moment. "How can I unfold into someone that I already am?" you might ask. As explained in the previous chapter, you have ideas, dreams, and visions that are given to you by True Essence that is desiring to be expressed. As human beings, we take on thought processes and beliefs from others that hinders us from expressing in our unique way. Because of this, there are tools and practices in place that support an individual in revealing their True, hence unfolding into who he already is. Borrowing from the Borgs, your resistance to your greatness and its unfolding is futile. Your resistance to all that wants to break through and reveal your true nature is futile. It is about accepting what True Essence knows about you and not conforming to what you thought your life would be based on the pain you have experienced in your life where previous beliefs and thought forms were created from. Those old habits and patterns can be transmuted to fulfill on the highest will of your life right now. Resistance is an inheritance blocker. It doesn't only block you; it blocks those who your life ministers to. When you hinder your unfolding, others are hindered and miss out, too.

WHY SAY "RESISTANCE IS FUTILE"?

AT THE END OF CHAPTER 1, I POSED A QUESTION, "Why are you resisting?" And by resisting, I mean fear. Resisting is allowing the feeling of fear to arise and take hold when experiencing a possibility or when there is a decision to become more of your true self – a commodity (which, by the way, is your birthright). Resisting is rejecting who the true self is, as a continuously unfolding being. It hinders any dreams, ideas, and visions from occurring. I remember asking myself that same question once I began to realize that I wasn't living to my full potential. I kept holding back myself because I was either worried about what other people thought or concerned that I wouldn't be accepted if I showed how grand I was. My mind was also peppered with what if thoughts: *What if I don't make it and my dreams, visions, and ideas don't work. What if my friends and family are right that I won't be* able to succeed in what I want to accomplish? I took all those thoughts into consideration, and I didn't realize that I was holding up the process of achieving my greatness. I didn't believe I could become the person of distinction that I had always wanted to be and earn the type of wealth and lifestyle I had always dreamed of. During his inaugural speech as President of the United States, made in the depths of the Great Depression, Franklin Delano Roosevelt declared, "The only thing we have to fear is fear itself." This simple statement made 80 years ago still rings true today. The only thing that can stop me is me, myself, and I. I took my focus off the greater picture and allowed myself to be deterred by what wasn't true about my life. I believed the opinions of others and the beliefs I created because of other's supposed thoughts about me. False understanding or resistant thoughts and beliefs took my attention away from focusing on my greater productivity.

The definition of *resistance* is, "a force that retards, hinders, or opposes motion." The forces that hinder motion are usually one's thoughts and beliefs about life including *if you fail, you're no good, you're not good enough to have..., you're too weak,* and *you're not smart enough* to mention a few. And let's not forget the beliefs and statements of those closest to you: *That didn't work for me, so it won't work for you. Our people are only productive at doing these types of things and working these types of jobs. They won't let you succeed. The only way you can get what you want is this way.* I have heard these statements before, and I have also believed them. I remember as early as grade school hearing friends repeat what adults told them about what was and wasn't possible. I'm amazed at the many things we were told and believed to be facts. The undeniable fact is that we are limitless beings; we don't have to be subjected to someone else's idea about how life should be lived.

There were moments when I didn't work on or even acknowledge my program, The Essential Peace of Life. I hindered opportunities from manifesting for myself and others through this program. At that time, I accepted my team, or upline's, feelings and beliefs on the program, and I believed I should feel the same way. I had someone very close to me tell me that I shouldn't think outside the box, and I held their words in such high esteem over my connection with True Essence. I forgot about myself and what was given to me by Essence. I didn't take into consideration that I, too, was a leader. I didn't realize that I wasn't going to be part of my upline forever. Yet I allowed that belief that my program wasn't possible, and that people didn't see me as a leader to take residence in my mind. I halted my rightful progression in life and surrendered to F.E.A.R – False Evidence About Reality. I accepted the reality of fear that wasn't true about me and my life instead of the reality that everything was working out for my good. I created a belief about myself and created my own hinderance. Did you see what I did there?

One of the definitions of futile is, "unimportant." Those negative thoughts and beliefs that I had were inconsequential in every way because they weren't based on the unique way my life was supposed to be lived. Yet I made them very important in my life. I allowed those thoughts and beliefs to be greater than my ideas and dreams that was given to me by Essence, which led me to procrastinate on what was placed inside me to do. Instead of trusting Source, I searched for other ways that may be more acceptable for others to feel proud of me. I didn't believe that I had everything available for me to succeed. I believed just the opposite and placed greatness on the backburner for mediocrity.

Together, the words *resistance* and *futile* provide the understanding that when you turn away from what is rightfully yours to express as your True self, difficult and uncomfortable paths are created as a result. It's akin to running a race, seeing the finish line, being ahead, then looking back, slowing down, and ultimately, losing the race. Now is the time to stop turning from the greatness that's trying to come forth and begin to make a conscious decision to move from a position of fear into your rightful destiny.

FEAR IS YOUR ALLY

For years, I reiterated that fear was a deterrent and that it had no place in anyone's life. I also attempted to figure out ways to suppress the energy of fear so that I could call myself courageous and strong. I kept trying to find different practices to fight or deny fear and was surprised that I couldn't find one because no one knew how to. Even when I would try to ignore fear, it would always find a way to reappear and would be stronger the second time around. It was during Practitioner Studies, a four-year licensed spiritual practitioner program offered through the Michael Bernard Beckwith School of Ministry at Agape International Spiritual Center, that I realized there is nothing to fight. There is, however, something to allow. Through the allowing, you will see the underlining reason for something like fear to appear in the moment. I began a practice where I approached all my fears as illusions based on thought forms and beliefs from other people and even my own understanding of my experiences. In this practice, I found out more about myself than ever, all because I dug deeper to the true reason under the initial emotion of fear.

When fear was a dominant part of my life, it was very unconstructive. I allowed myself to work jobs that I didn't like and didn't find joy in because I believed that I couldn't earn more somewhere else. I believed that since I had been on my job for so long, that I needed to be patient and wait my turn for a raise (despite the feeling in my body that something better awaited). I stayed in relationships with people who didn't respect me, who didn't want to put forth the effort in the relationship, and who didn't like me for me, all for the sake of not being alone. I didn't move forward on various ideas and visions because I didn't know what would happen if I executed them. All of this and more took place because I didn't know my position as a Divine being and who I am. A lot of things I endured was because I allowed fear to have prominence over how I lived. It was all about keeping myself from feeling pain and fitting in. No matter how hard I tried, I didn't fit in. Deep down, I knew that it was possible to earn the amount of income that I wanted. I knew the type of people I wanted in my life and joyous relationships could be for me. I knew how to stand tall. I decided to pick me first and began to affirm myself, even when fear was present. I knew that I was a leader by right and a great person because I was created by True Essence. Besides, Essence don't make any junk (bad grammar intentional). Yet knowing this wasn't enough; I had to act. Through action, I realized I couldn't beat or get away from fear, I had to face it.

I have the right to have joy in my life – to have it and experience it as my life. I began to look at what was causing fear in the moments when I wanted to feel joy. This pivot is when I began to allow fear to be my ally. From this point, I allowed fear to show me what was in me that didn't allow me to move from my true nature, which is Joy. I posed a self-inquiry: *What process can open me fully and completely and be a daily practice whenever I had fear moments?*

Fear became my ally because it allowed me to go underneath the surface illusion of an issue and see what I neglected and what was longing for love. Fear had done me a huge favor. Had it not been for fear, I wouldn't have noticed a deep-seated program was there. I wouldn't have taken the time to bring it to my surface mind to see what created the illusion of the problem. Without using that signal to my benefit, I would have remained stuck in resistance.

A LIMITLESS UNIVERSE

THERE IS AN ULTIMATE CONNECTION THAT LETS ME know that I already have what it takes to succeed. In his book *Psychogenesis*, Jack Addington writes, "Man can do whatever he is able to conceive in his mind, receive in his consciousness, expect with assurance, and accept in actual experience. The Universe does not set limitations. We set them by our own belief about ourselves." Stated in my words: You can conceive whatever you think and want to become, because you are part of True Essence, which only wants success for all its expressions. Comforting, right? And even still, there are moments of resisting our greatness because of the limitations we place on ourselves because we don't have a proper relationship with fear. And you know what? We have no reason to be afraid. We all can let fear show us what is holding us back from moving forward with our dreams and ideas. When the deep-seated belief or reasoning reveals itself, and is showered with love, then there are no limitations to what can be accomplished. "God has not given us the spirit of fear, yet of power, and of love, and of a sound mind." (2 Timothy 1:7). Having a sound and open mind allows fear to be your ally, gives you the power to keep it from having a lasting effect, and infused you with the love that helps it dissolve.

With a sound and open mind, you will see more clearly what is really happening and a whole new world will open for you. Remember, whatever has been lost will be given to you again, because nothing is ever lost in the Universe. It will become easier to be in the flow of living a full life and seeing fear for what it truly is.

My love for speaking and helping others assisted me in maneuvering through the ups and downs that came along with fulfilling my dreams and ideas. Permitting fear to be my ally instead of my nemesis allowed me to see my productivity in a situation and from there, release what was deeply embedded in my subconscious. This process kept me on my toes and ready for anything and I began taking everything as a learning experience. I expected an abundance of opportunities to come my way. Not only did I believe this, yet I also started to live as if it was already happening. As a result, I heard Spirit more and my life upgraded exponentially.

MISTAKES ARE PRODUCTIVE

WHEN I WAS IN RESISTANCE MODE, I STUNTED MYSELF from expressing my greatness and from doing what I was excited to do as Spirit. Consequently, there were learning experiences that had to take place and they presented as mistakes. Mistake means, "An error in action or calculation caused by insufficient knowledge." Making mistakes allowed me to see how I could've handled things differently to achieve an optimum outcome. The great thing about making mistakes is that they can be rectified. Making the same mistake would only mean that I didn't learn or listen from it the first time and didn't take the time to fully understand what was really happening. That would also be in the line of the definition of insanity – doing the same thing over again and expecting a different result. At times, I wanted to give up completely because the fear of getting hurt and feeling the pain of the mistakes.

I can remember when I first began my journey to become a paid motivational speaker. I received some information from a fellow speaker friend of mine to start making cold calls to different agencies, schools and youth centers that was in my target market. After receiving the information, I was gung-ho to get started on my first pitch, yet I didn't because of the fear of making a mistake. I didn't know what to say and how to say it. I would begin to make a phone call and once on the phone, forget to ask for the person who makes the decisions to book speakers. Even when I did get on the line with the person I needed to speak to, I would stumble over my words when talking. Sometimes, I just stared aimlessly at the phone, wanting to call, yet too afraid that I'd make a mistake and blow my chance of getting in the door. I became extremely stagnant and once again buried myself in working a job that I didn't enjoy. I allowed my resistance to making mistakes become important, which slowed my dream of speaking in front of millions of people and sharing my message, The Essential Peace of Life. Then I remembered the advice I was given when I began proposing my motivational speaking business: *Stop sitting on this and move, because faith without works is dead.* In other words, I could want my business to grow all I want and see myself speaking in front of millions of people, yet if I did nothing to get myself in the door and on a stage, it wouldn't matter how much I envisioned it, it would remain a dream.

I went online to search for the numbers of local schools, and I went to local community centers to set up appointments to schedule speaking engagements. I introduced myself to the directors and even the assistants and asked if they knew anyone who was looking for a talented motivational speaker. Because of my diligence, I got a meeting with a director of a community center whose name was Jim. I bombed terribly on my initial proposal at the first meeting. I wasn't prepared. I didn't have the information he requested, and I didn't know how to respond to his questions. Jim knew and understood that I was trying my best and graciously gave me some tips. He stated that when someone asks me how much my services cost to have my price and stick to it no matter what the person feels about it. He also advised that it was best to have in writing my topics, the benefits of my presentation, and how the organization hiring me would benefit. I wrote down his advice immediately and left to properly prepare my presentation. Thankfully, Jim graciously extended me another chance to meet with him.

The mistakes I made with Jim ended up being a huge blessing and, in this case, fear was a true ally. I received valuable feedback from a generous person who saw my desire to be a blessing to others. Because I was willing to meet with Jim, even when I wasn't fully prepared, I received the guidance and insight that would serve me in future meetings. I went back a day later and was more prepared. I didn't get the time and amount of money that I initially requested, yet I was invited to speak at an engagement that Jim was hosting later that week (and got paid for it). If I didn't take the time to make those mistakes, I would not have had the learning experience that I got from Jim. I could have believed the negative chatter and allowed the mistakes to be a barrier instead of steppingstones as they later were.

THE DEEPEST POWER WITHIN

WHEN I DIDN'T LET RESISTANCE TAKE OVER MY DREAM, I began to see the power that I had within myself and my ability to co-create with Essence. Not only did I allow resistance to be my ally, I opened to Essence, trusted the guidance I received, and made connections with someone who could help me enhance my dream. If I allowed the fear of my proposal not being received to stop me, I would have allowed resistance to win and I wouldn't have received what I rightfully deserved. I wouldn't have learned from my mistake and wouldn't have been encouraged to research more information I needed to have a better meeting with prospects.

I'm reminded of the passage, "Our Deepest Fear,"

which I read in the book *A Return to Love* by Marianne Williamson:

"Our deepest fear is not that we are inadequate. Our deepest fear is that we are powerful beyond measure. It is our light, not our darkness that most frightens us. We ask ourselves, who am I to be brilliant, gorgeous, talented, and fabulous? Actually, who are you not to be? You are a child of God. Your playing small does not serve the world. There is nothing enlightened about shrinking so that other people won't feel insecure around you. We are all meant to shine, as children do. We were born to make manifest the glory of God that is within us. It's not just in some of us; it's in everyone. And as we let our own light shine, we unconsciously give other people permission to do the same. As we are liberated from our own fear, our presence automatically liberates others."

When we realize that we have nothing to fear at all, we also remember who and whose we are. We all have the same Power and Presence that is the foundation of our lives. This foundation has already created the path of success and accomplishments for us. Our charge is to support the heart in moving confidently in the direction of manifesting our dreams and visions. Even when momentum seems to slow, it presents a beautiful opportunity to regroup, come back to center, refocus on Spirit, and move towards your rightful glory, which is the glory of the Great One within. There is no need to worry about the inconsequential nature of resistance, because you have what it takes to make it from True Essence within. All that Essence has is yours. You own it right now and all you need do is allow it.

Williamson's "Our Deepest Fear," reproduced above, establishes that we are great beings with unlimited abilities to do and receive whatever we want. You are a commodity with awesome potential. Being a great, upstanding, and highly qualified person is your rightful inheritance from True Essence, as a gift for living on this planet. It's not a privilege, it is your right. There is no fear great enough to stop you; use it as an opportunity to prove the naysayers and the negative chatter in your head wrong. During the time I experienced seizures, I had moments where I wanted to play small to ensure people would "like" me and want to be around me. I developed a lot of internal negative chatter because I didn't want to disobey my mother, even though she didn't fully understand the severity of the seizures. My mother didn't want to appear like she wasn't being a good mother; she didn't want people to believe that she didn't have control of her children. That was a belief that had been passed down from generation to generation. I had so many questions as a child and as you can probably suspect, I masqueraded around as if everything was OK to uphold someone else's false belief. I wore that mask for many years of my life. I did a great job appeasing my mother even though I desired to yell out how I truly felt. I knew doing so would dishonor her. I resisted my true nature for the sake of upholding what I thought was acceptable. This masquerade also affected other relationships I was in. I interacted with others and they with me based on my mask. I unconsciously created a standard without knowing it by taking on an idea that was given to me as a child. Even with all the work I've done around releasing the mask, some people still don't know how to relate to me because of the mask I had worn for so many years.

Even though I was the culprit that dimmed my own light, I knew that I was better than the charade I was keeping up. I was better than what I was holding on to. It took a great chunk of my life and daily forgiveness work to release the resistance I had. I learned how to be a kind person. I also learned how to create boundaries and stand up for what I believe in when it comes to me and my life. That and numerous other learning moments have presented themselves for my growth, yet there were some things that I didn't have a grasp on. If nothing else, I always knew and felt during that time of my life that I had Essence to guide and support me. I was open to hearing the voice within giving me direction even in the times when I didn't listen.

Once you tap into that knowing, you unconsciously give other people permission to do the same, like Marianne Williamson said, and liberation becomes a daily lifestyle. Despite my bumpy start, I didn't do so bad. I ended up in California, at Agape International Spiritual Center, working closely with Rev. Michael and other practitioners and ministers. All of this was because I didn't give up on myself and I kept going, no matter what it took. There was a video on Facebook I watched where a young man, who was mentally challenged, stood in front of a church filled with people singing the Negro hymn, "Amazing Grace." Although he sang off key and didn't know all the words, he encouraged others around him to sing. Unconcerned about what others thought, the man sang his heart out, just like he heard others sing and he was being his full and authentic self. He didn't dim his light. What I saw in that video was someone who wasn't resisting his productivity that was for him to share. He didn't act small because he didn't know the words to the song; he shined bright because he was willing to do what it took to be encouraging to those around him. All thoughts are from True Essence itself and those very actions became the outcome of the Divine's glory.

I have a request for you: Please stop resisting your abilities to create your own business or different avenues of income. Please stop making excuses for not doing what it takes to move up in your current job. Please stop neglecting to help those who may benefit from your skills and expertise. Whatever you've always wanted to be and do and, most importantly, what True Essence has planned for you to be and do, please do it.

CAUTION DOESN'T MEAN STOP

It's alright at times to be cautious when moving forward on your ideas and dreams. Most of us are used to working or doing for someone else that it feels foreign and out of place to do something for ourselves. Yet don't let this new feeling keep you from stretching beyond your comfort zone. For example, I have had grand ideas that if applied would completely turn my life around for the better, yet I found myself wanting to stay stuck in what I was doing at the time because it was familiar to me.

My father and Uncle Joe (my mother's brother)

came from different time periods and their way of living was completely different than how people live today. I wanted to do more creative things that would allow me to be an inspirational speaker, even though I felt I was in line to learn the family business of being a pastor. I only had the example of my father and my uncle, and they both worked and ran a church together. My father would work on Sunday at times because he would get paid more and continued to encourage me to do the same, yet that wasn't what I wanted to do with my life. I wanted to be a speaker like my Uncle Joe. Yet when I confided in my uncle that I wanted to be an inspirational speaker like Les Brown, he told me that it wouldn't be profitable or successful. In short, he advised me to stay in the box. And for a time, I did. Eventually, I would miss Sunday services and felt terrible because I felt like I was missing out on my training. I felt bad because I held off my passion to please my uncle and as you see, that didn't last long. Yes, my father and uncle did what they needed to do for themselves and their family at the time, yet there was something unique developing within me that was for me to do. I had to do the work to make myself available.

At the time, my familiar was mediocrity and stagnancy. When I did decide to follow my dream of being an inspirational speaker, I held on to what my father and uncle told me, and it kept me from fully embracing new opportunities. When I tried to maintain the mindset of getting a better paying job, I was cautious about going back to college because I had failed miserably in the past. I didn't think I had it in me to become a great student and exceptional learner. I was cautious about writing this book and producing the Peace is Essential to Life program, because when I first shared about it, it wasn't received with enthusiasm like I imagined. If I had allowed my caution to become my fear and never allow it to be my ally, I wouldn't have acquired the success that I now enjoy. And while I'm certain there will be more cautious moments I experience in life, I have the tools now and the assurance to allow it all to work out on my behalf.

My Uncle Mike, my mother's brother, shared a quote by Neale Donald Walsch with me after an intriguing conversation on a section I was writing in this book. "Caution is natural, yet fear is not. Do not give in to fear, yet do not abandon caution. It is a balancing act. Caution is what causes you to look both ways before crossing the street. Fear is what keeps you frozen on the curb forever. You know the difference. You can feel it. If you're "stuck" right now, you're probably into fear. Get out of there. You've already looked both ways. Now cross the street, for heaven's sake. The cars have long since gone. The coast is clear. Your only obstacle now is your own mind." Neale was right: We already know what is needed to achieve what is rightfully ours. Moving forward means trusting that everything is working already. When we worry, it slows down and prolongs the thing we desire – even when the coast is clear for us to receive it. Admittedly, I was very afraid at one point because I didn't know how I could get by in life if I did move forward with the idea of being an inspirational speaker. What would it look, feel, and be like to have that type of life? Who would support me and believe that what I was doing was important and will help others? I had to take that step of faith and not allow fear to take over. Did I have what it takes? Will speaking take care of my bills and food, and someday, my family? Even with these thoughts and cautions, I had to keep moving forward to get what is rightfully mine. Rev. Michael Bernard Beckwith once said, "The how doesn't matter; what matters is that you're open and available to what Spirit has for you to do – and to follow it without delay." It's OK to be cautious if the caution doesn't prevent you from moving forward.

Moving forward from caution is to align oneself to the Source within by creating an agreement that the ideas, dreams, and visions are more important than the negative thoughts that attempt to prevent them from manifesting. Isaiah 26:3 says, "Thou wilt keep him in perfect peace, whose mind is stayed on thee: because he trusts in thee." The very Power within will not allow Itself to be blocked of its right to shine. It encourages us to do what it takes to allow It to shine through our unique expressions. It is wonderful to know that True Essence is always there, and always ready and willing to do what it takes to give us an opening to be the Peace that we rightfully are. When we are ready to acknowledge Its presence and keep our mind on It, we will experience peace and more.

DEEPER IN THE GROOVE (D.I.G)

I AM AMAZED AT THE AMOUNT OF TIME, EFFORT, AND energy that I put into believing what someone thought to be true for me. I had to go through a process of digging out the negative thoughts and beliefs that allowed fear to have power. I had to dig deep under the feeling of fear to remove the thoughts and beliefs that no longer supported my way of living. I had to go *Deeper in the Groove.*

The Deeper in the Groove process is very simple. First, bring your awareness to the issue and allow yourself to be fully present with it. Then, close your eyes and ask the issue what the real reason for it is. (Trust me you will get an answer.) Then, thank the issue, love it away, and allow the true belief or thought to have its 15 seconds of fame as well. This is a great time to be open to possibly more than one belief or thought. If that occurs, be gentle with yourself and take the necessary time to see if you're willing to deal with more or not. Again, take the time to thank that belief or thought and love it away because it no longer fits your way of life. If a person comes to your awareness that you allowed to plant the belief or if it was just you, this is the moment to forgive that person or yourself. This is another form of release because the energy of resentment doesn't help growth. Then affirm what is the truth of who you are and what you are capable of being and doing. Affirm that you are created to do whatever Essence has created you to do and more, and there is nothing against you, only for you.

By working with the Deeper in the Groove process, your mind will open and willing to do what it takes to fulfill on your dreams and ideas. I had to create daily declarations that reminded myself constantly that the message I had was worth telling people. I assured myself that I was productive enough to tell whoever would listen about how *The Essential Peace of Life* could be a successful and beneficial part of their lives. I had to realize that True Essence gave me something valuable and I also had to believe that even though no one else had my back, True Essence did. I did whatever it took to reshape my mind and transform the beliefs and thought processes so that I could function as the true energetic conduit of Spirit. I had to D.I.G. out the thoughts and beliefs that I allowed to remain dormant and take up space about me and my life. Once I made it my mission to D.I.G., I built up my confidence to pull *The Essential Peace of Life* back out again and revamp it to make it more of what people needed to hear. And now you have it in your hands and people around the world will have it as well.

Because of these techniques, I have practiced how to shift to a more uplifting and productive way of being. No matter what, I realized that I had nothing to fear anymore. I allowed the beliefs and thoughts that no longer worked with me to surface, and I let them go. I stopped resisting my productiveness that was working on my behalf and moved in faith that my ideas, dreams, and visions were already available and done.

Fear is never a motivator for something to be done right. It will always come across as a challenge because the person is running away from something. Their focus isn't about getting the job done to complete perfection, yet getting the job done so they aren't punished. A motivator based in love, peace, joy, and compassion will always get the desired result because of the intention behind it. Fear doesn't accomplish anything; it only brings anger, turmoil, and resistance. Love, Joy, Peace, and Compassion will get the desired outcome and create an enjoyable environment.

Is there any reason to allow anyone or anything to tell you that you can't do something? Now is the time to believe that you can. Who told you that you couldn't? The Universe didn't, so why are you listening?

3

PAIN HELPS CREATE YOUR ENVIRONMENT

During my adolescent years, I thought that where I lived, what I wore, and how I spoke determined my true status in life and if I would be accepted by others. I felt that I was better than others because I could almost get whatever I wanted. My belief was that life was wonderful to me and my family; however, I didn't have the complete package. Many of those years I held on to false beliefs that I received as a child and on the inside, I felt abandoned. Even at that time in my life I was still dealing with my pain and trying to find ways to subside it to feel excited about myself and what I was experiencing. I was trying to ignore that which was bothering and hindered me the most and didn't find out how it could serve me for my productivity. Yet no one could tell me anything; I felt that I was better and on a different level than most people. I felt others couldn't touch me because I had a better life – at least on the outside.

As I grew older, I realized that I didn't have it as well as when I lived with my parents. I had to have a job that supported the type of lifestyle I had with my parents. I had to trust it was possible to obtain that type of status if I so choose to. Of course, my parents wanted me to have what they had; they even wanted me to have better. There was something inside me that prevented me from opening to the possibilities that my life had to offer. I didn't have the tools to transform the pain of my youth into something that would assist me in manifesting the dreams, ideas, and visions that I had. As I tried to get things right and find my own way, I didn't get far at all. I had ideas that came to me from Spirit, and I didn't know how to harness that information and make it my reality.

I started to read stories of some of my favorite athletes, inspirational speakers, and musical artists, and realized that their beginnings seemed far worse than mine. Despite their earlier years, they worked hard and believed in themselves, regardless of the obstacles they faced. That's when I began to understand that my environment didn't determine who I was and what I could become. My environment only personifies the type of lifestyle and living conditions that I was in at the time and that wasn't even from my own hard work. I had it mixed up when I thought that what I had on the outside and where I lived were who I was. I didn't work at all for what I had growing up – that was my parents' doing. When I stepped into the "real world" it was different and the house and cars that I bragged about were all gone. I would make daily trips to my parents' house just so I could get that feeling of having again. The real power that I had, and didn't realize was important, was what was inside of me. This power and presence were my very life. This was the Essence I believed those athletes, inspirational speakers, and musicians tapped into, which helped them express their truest nature.

You might be wondering, "If where I live and what I have aren't important then what is?" I believe the most important thing in life is that everyone is full and funded by an Unlimited Source that knows all, sees all, and is totally active, all powerful, and everywhere present. This Essence is what I believe we all are. It is the very power that provides what is necessary to accomplish the dream, ideas, and visions that are within. We are to do what it takes to learn the practices that help manifest the vision. We are to practice being one with Spirit through mediation, prayer, and affirmations, which will open us to the power that's already within. Practicing these disciplines will maintain and empower the process of your unfoldment. Being in the flow of what Spirit wants for you and not what would make you cool or accepted in another's eyes is what gives you the greatest feeling. There will always be a new car that looks better than the old one. Someone will always have something to say about what they think is best for you and how that best should be experienced. Yet, the only approval that is warranted is your own. All that matters is that you feel wonderful about what will help you sustain and maintain your true nature, and that's peace.

WHAT IS ENVIRONMENT?

THE WORD *ENVIRONMENT* MEANS, "CONDITIONS OR influences; surroundings; external factors surrounding and affecting a given organism at any time; the social and cultural force that shapes the life of a person or a population." I believe how a person thinks plays a part in creating their environment, especially when it comes to accomplishing their visions, ideas, and dreams. The role that pain and hurt play in someone's environment is huge as well. Enduring the trauma from the past of an adult loved one that never knew how to maneuver it and passed it on to young people in their lives. No one is limited to their physical environment and the narrative that environment might represent. Your environment, although it plays a part, does not dictate what is truly possible in your life and what can be achieved. I had to come to this understanding in my life. I later realized that there was something greater for me to accomplish that went beyond the steps my parents took to create the environment they enjoyed. I, too, had ideas and dreams that I needed to work on that would open doors to the environment that I desired to create. I didn't have time to focus on where I was, I had to begin to focus on where I wanted to be and who I wanted to become.

Everyone can create room to receive an expansion of greatness despite where they live, what others think of them, and what they do or don't have. In the book *Life Visioning,* Michael Bernard Beckwith writes, "We as spiritual beings are endogenous, which means proceeding from within, derived internally, and originated from within." After reading this passage, I realized that is it a human tendency to waste precious energy and attention basing our perceptions on our external surroundings. There are so many people who spend more energy on material possessions that can't add any value to their life. To truly succeed and win in life, the attention must be turned from outside to within.

Making decisions and moving from within is something that cannot be taken from you. Jobs end, relationships come and go, yet your ability to tune into Divine Essence can never be hindered or removed from you. Everything you need for this journey is right where you are. No matter the pain and or circumstances you have been born into and how life may have been like for you, True Essence within gives you everything you need to make it. Please don't make the error in believing that your environment determines how life will be for you. In truth, your life can be magnificent even with a rough or rocky start. Yet first, you must believe this and place yourself in a position for this to manifest as true in your life.

CREATING THE ENVIRONMENT
WANTED IS POSSIBLE

I HAVE WATCHED AN INNUMERABLE AMOUNT OF PEOPLE fulfill their dreams. Whether it's playing sports, making music, paintings in the art galleries, performing in movies or plays and motivating millions of people, these individuals have and continue to fulfill their heart's desires. And they all have come from various environments. Whether they hailed from the fearful projects of New York City, sexually, mentally, and or physically abusive home, a cattle ranch in Colorado, or a suburban neighborhood in Phoenix, Arizona, they all at one point said, "I want to do that!" and did it. Once their minds were made up, they followed through with actions – such as taking classes and practicing – that helped them perfect their craft. They joined teams and groups and welcomed mentorship to hone their skills. Some wanted their dream to happen so much that they worked hard and moved to regions halfway across the continent that supported their passionate crafts (just like I did). These people never gave up on what they wanted to accomplish and have found their way to the dream.

I once read a story that I'll share here about a woman named Dani Johnson. Dani grew up with parents who used drugs. While living at home with her parents, she was abused sexually and physically for many years. At the age of 21, Dani moved to Hawaii where she worked as a waitress and lived in her car. Even though she left her physical environment, she maintained the same attitude her parents had and started to drink alcohol and use drugs. Dani despised her life, so much so that she wanted to end it by drowning herself in the ocean. She didn't feel like her life was going to get any better. After several attempts, she heard a voice say to her, "Pick up your mat and walk." In that moment, she lost the urge to continue to do drugs. As Dani was leaving the beach, she heard two conflicting voices in her head. One voice said, "This is not what is intended for your life; you shouldn't be drinking. There is more to life." The other voice said, "You're a failure. You're a loser. You're filthy and worse than your parents. Drive this car into the ocean." The next morning, she made a conscious decision to change her life and how she made money. From that choice, she started a business where she sold weight loss programs to people. That business developed and after two years, she sold it and became a millionaire. After enduring many problems with her environment, she did what it took to overcome those problems. She became a multimillionaire and helps millions of people do the same.

The Essential Pain and Peace of Life

Dani Johnson was born in a hurtful and painful environment. Even though she moved away, she mimicked her parents' lifestyle and almost ended her life. Dani made a choice to not allow her past environment to dictate how she would live moving forward. She eventually listened to a still, small voice – the Source within – had a battle with her past and what is possible and made the proper changes to better her life. Because of her resilience and newfound belief in herself, she is now traveling the world, teaching people how they can change their lives for the better, just like she did.

No matter what, it is always possible to transform into and experience something greater. It doesn't have to be as rough as Dani's experience or as wonderful as I thought I had growing up. My point is that we're awesome beings who live on this Earth who each have the power to reach our potential in life. What I know as fact is that there is so much more than meets the eye when we open to the infinite possibilities within us. Once I looked past my environment, I opened to greater and broader ideas. I went through a hard time with my parents and felt that I wasn't heard. I wanted to give up, had lost inspiration, and even threatened to take my life just to get some attention. Yet Spirit had other plans. Ideas, dreams, and visions kept coming to me. The more these things came to me, the less I could focus on getting attention from others. Instead, I became excited about what was to come and what was possible. Something greater and wonderful was wanting, waiting, and available to be co-created.

I'm a huge World Wrestling Entertainment fan. I noticed after reading a few bios of my favorite wrestlers that many had college degrees and worked in other professions before becoming wrestling superstars. Take Dwayne "The Rock" Johnson for instance. The Rock is a third-generation wrestler (his grandfather was Peter Maivia and his father Rocky Johnson) and got his start as an athlete in college. He went on to play professional football. When he didn't make it as a big-time football player and left the game with only $7 in his pocket, The Rock thought his only way out was to become a wrestler. After a gimmick chance, he became one of the greatest W.W.E. champions and superstars of all time. After several years of wrestling, he transitioned onto the big screen, becoming the highest-paid movie star in W.W.E. history. He doesn't have to wrestle again if he doesn't want to; however, because of the millions (and millions) of The Rock fans, he continues to make appearances ever so often. And still the hottest ticket around. If you ever get the chance watch, "Young Rock," it will give you a deeper dive into his life.

Then there is David Otunga, a Harvard-educated

lawyer who practiced law for a little while before he rose to prominence on a reality TV show called, *I Love New York*. He appeared as a possible suitor to a woman named "New York" (real name Tiffany Pollard) who was searching for love from a pool of 50 eligible bachelors. He went on to meet and marry Jennifer Hudson, an Academy Award-winning actress and singer. David is currently a W.W.E. wrestler and handles some legal work and commentary for the company sometimes. Who knows what is next for this young man?

Shaquille O'Neal was born to a single mother and later raised by Phillip Author Harrison, a Sargent in the U.S. Army who loved Shaq and his mom very much. Philip helped Shaquille go from being a class clown who was failing in school to a dominating collegiate basketball player at Louisiana State University to one of the 50 greatest NBA players of all time. Though those antics as a class clown never left him, he diversified that energy into talent by appearing in movies before his NBA career took off. He was also a musical artist and was featured in video games produced by Sega and Nintendo called Shaq-Fu. Now retired, Shaq is a sports analyst for TNT, part-time cop, and has his Doctorate in Human Resource Development, He promised his mother that he would continue his education because education was a priority in his family.

Through the above examples, I hope you see that there is an ability to accomplish whatever you choose to do. Life is not limited to only one direction. No matter what origins a person may have started from, there is always something wonderful for them. Notice I didn't mention anything about the type of homes these successful people started in or the style of clothes they wore or the type of cars they may have driven. What's true is that each person came from different environments and pursued their dream. They never gave up on themselves and I believe that you, too, share this same ability to follow your dream.

Life is what you make it. It's not good or bad, it just is. And every choice that is made is backed by the Universe which can be altered into something wonderful and simply marvelous. We have the power to change what we do and how we show up and the best part about your life is that it's not for anyone else to dictate. We are beings of the Holy One who get to live the experience as humans here on this Earth. If there is a great environment to be experienced, everyone has the power to create it, and it is based on everyone's unique pattern. As you grow, your environment will grow along with you. When a person grows mentally and spiritually, so does the capacity to which life is experienced and one's ability to call forth that which is not as though it already is. So, get ready for the exponential growth.

CHOOSE YOUR SURROUNDINGS WISELY

IN HIS BOOK, *GOLDEN RULES: THE LOST WRITINGS*, Napoleon Hill states, "We begin to see the importance of selecting our environment with the greatest of care, because environment is the mental feeding ground out of which the food that goes into our minds is extracted. Environment supplies the food and the materials out of which we create thoughts, and habit crystallizes these materials into permanency." Since the goal is to create thriving and productive environments, it is important to be around high-vibration, high-energy, and high-minded individuals who will affirm the type of environment you desire to thrive in and from. It is your right as a being of Spirit to recognize that once you begin to uplevel your way of being, it becomes impossible to return to an old way of being and doing because it will no longer be comfortable. A new way of living will form, and you will become like Neo from the Matrix, who began to see binary code (an example of an Infinite, All-

Inclusive, All-Providing environment and a limitless, ever-expanding existence that is truly who you are). As you begin to see, you expand beyond what you once believed possible, allowing the very Essence of life itself to multiple infinitely as you.

Everyone has the power to choose how his or her environment can be and the people who are part of it. With this stated, the environment need not only be physical or structural, yet it can also be the type of people you associate with that creates your environment. I never knew why certain individuals were placed in my life or how long they would stay in my life. If my thoughts toward that person were based on how they looked, then I may miss the opportunity to grow and excel in an area of life that the person judged could help me in. I could have lost a partner and potentially, a true friend. My environment could take longer to be created because I wasn't open to a person because of how they looked. I'm reminded of something my Uncle Joe Peeler would say often, "Be careful how you treat people because they could be angels unaware."

When I started college in 1995, I met Bob, a cool dude and we hit it off right from the start. His parents owned a brokerage firm, and they lived on the eastside of Buffalo, not totally upscale, yet it was comfortable. Bob and I shared the same vision of owning a music production company. We agreed that he would be the sole owner and I would be his partner, as well as the singer-songwriter. We searched for people with different talents who could help build the brand and be part of our company, "Ruff Buff Productions." As time passed, I noticed how Bob manipulated his environment to fit how he wanted things to play out. I felt that Bob didn't understand what true friendship was and because of that, he treated people as if they were beneath him. He didn't think they were on his level, and he began to discredit people based on their looks and their environment. I was amazed at how he would befriend someone and turn on them in the same breath. He projected a perfect life externally, yet internally, he needed help. I began to see that things weren't what he said they were, yet I never called him on it; I was glad to have a friend to hang with. I was going through my own illusions of issues from the pain I was carrying, so anything to take my mind off of what was happening to me. And although I saw how he treated others, I never thought he would treat me the same. I was his right-hand man after all.

Bob placed people in compromising positions and questioned their loyalty. It got to the point where he felt he could coerce others into being what he thought they should be. From my vantage, he didn't believe they had a mind of their own. The moment he attempted to force an opinion or coerce me in a situation, I removed myself from him and the company. Some of our past associates no longer wanted to be around him. Things got so bad with Bob's relationships that eventually, he moved out of town. No matter where he went and who he associated with, his behavior and how he treated people followed him. He didn't see the lesson that was right in front of him to learn, which was how to be a true friend.

My relationship with Bob taught me to not judge a book by its cover. I believed Bob had a an awesome heart and was a wonderful person, yet I also believed that how he treated was a direct correlation to how he felt about himself. Maya Angelo, a Nobel Prize-winning poet, and author once said, "When someone shows you who they are, believe them." I live by this quote and take it into consideration every time I meet new people. I no longer look at how a person looks, what they wear, and where they are from; rather, I listen intently and watch their actions and reactions. It amazes me that Bob didn't learn this lesson before things started to go haywire in his life. Maybe one day he will.

LOVE YOURSELF TO BUILD BOUNDARIES

I LOVE WHO I AM. ADMITTEDLY, IT TOOK TIME TO GET to the point where I could say that because of the power I gave to other people's perceptions of me. Letting the pain of my past take control of how I show up in the world. Just like I allowed the pain to do and act whatever and however the energy wanted to express itself through me and so I allowed that same energy to happen to me from other people. When I learned to love myself, I leaned in more to what is trying to be communicated to me when the pain of my past would surface and what I needed to be strong and gentle with myself, to become more open to my true self as Peace. I began to become more comfortable with who I am and allowing myself to speak up and stand firm in my decision making for and about myself. Loving myself would also help people around me to better understand me. From there, it was their choice to love me or like me for me. This allowed me to have boundaries and helped me shape how I wanted my environment to be.

Boundaries wasn't something I paid much attention to or even knew about growing up because I wasn't taught to have them. My mother did the best she could when it came to my health (seizures). Even though I didn't have control over them, I tried my best to stay in my mother's good graces so that she would love me. I didn't have boundaries. Not only was I attempting to please my mother, yet I was also trying to please my relatives and people in general. This way of being attracted some users and friendship abusers. All of it was based on a learned behavior that spawned from a belief I held around relating to people. I wanted people to be around me, yet I didn't think boundaries would help me. If anything, I thought having boundaries would scare people away, which was the last thing I wanted. I later noticed that not having boundaries hurt me more than others. I also began to see that other people had boundaries and they didn't hesitate to exercise those boundaries with me. I noticed that I sacrificed myself by putting up with certain behaviors just to have friends or acquaintances. I put my self-love and respect in jeopardy that I wouldn't feel alone.

When I hung around Bob, it took time for me to realize that I needed to have boundaries. In retrospect, I was putting myself in danger at that time of my life by doing things I normally wouldn't do just for the sake of having a friend. I even got jumped by some of Bob's acquaintances over an issue that could have been solved through a conversation. And Bob did nothing to help. That was the final straw for me, and I set boundaries in our relationship. Eventually, I stopped associating with him altogether. I began to learn what my self-worth was and became clear on what and who I wanted in my environment moving forward. When I made that decision to have boundaries, things around me changed. I realized if someone wanted to get to know me, they had to respect my world. First, I had to model this through how I treated and respected myself. I am one with the Unlimited Life, so it would behoove me to check the way I treated myself and my alignment with my true Self. The more I respected myself, the more I would receive this same respect from those around me.

How do you move through the mental challenge of creating boundaries? First, you must be OK with knowing and being who you are. There is no way to create boundaries or even be comfortable around anyone else if you aren't comfortable with yourself. The love, joy, peace, and harmony that you experience with yourself is far more potent and important than what you would have with anyone else. If you want things to change, you must be the change that you want. This must be so clear and second nature to you that you won't waiver unless you feel the compromise is necessary. Second, listen to the still, small voice within. When you are guided by Source Energy, you are also guided in a way that is unique to you. When things seem difficult, go within via meditation and prayer, and allow yourself to be fully directed by that Source within. Third, affirm to yourself that you already have what you want and that your boundaries will be honored, because you honor them also. Affirm to yourself, "I am in a pleasant environment that is divinely designed for all, including me, to respect and enjoy." This will open the pathway for those who are meant to be in your environment. Lastly, speak up. There are ways to say something to someone without being harsh, yet it is not up to you to be responsible for how they take it. Learning to stand firm and speak on what I would and would not accept has demonstrated back to me self-love and respect. When you speak up, you are showing to the other person that you value yourself and you love yourself. Remember, this takes practice and is a work in progress so be patient with yourself and others as they adjust to this new you.

PERSONAL DEVELOPMENT

THERE WAS A TIME IN MY LIFE WHEN I DIDN'T THINK I needed additional help. I believed I had it together. Thankfully, I realized that wasn't the case. I also thought that once I learned information and it worked for me that I was done. In my mind, I made it and there was nothing more for me to learn. I didn't realize that I was still holding onto pains and beliefs that were dictating and controlling my way of living. There were a lot of areas of my life that needed some tightening up, understanding, and a proper release. So, instead of spending a lot of time doing things that didn't enhance my life, I started to seek things that would help me unfold to my greater yet to be. When I was a member of the multi-level marketing group, they were really big on personal development as a way to help sell more product. I noticed that when I didn't get the desired outcome or sales that I would do a self-inventory to see where I could improve. This inventory relayed invaluable information that helped me to adjust how I interacted with potential customers, thus increasing my sales. The same concept is true when growing spiritually. Benjamin Franklin once said, "If I had 4 hours to chop down a tree, I'd spend 3 hours sharpening my ax and one hour chopping the tree." This quote emphasizes the importance of adequate preparation, which is gained when you are self-aware, and strengthened through personal development.

 In 2003, the leader of the multi-level marketing team I was part of gave me a book by Dale Carnegie, *How to Win Friends and Influence People*. My whole environment changed reading that book, and I learned how to become a more well-rounded person, in my personal and business relationships. I later invested in more self-help books, audios, and e-books including *Think and Grow Rich* by Napoleon Hill, *As A Man Thinketh* by James Allen, *Developing the Leader Within You* by John C. Maxwell, *and Rich Dad Poor Dad* by Robert Kiyosaki. I didn't just read those books; I practiced the advice. I learned that learning wasn't a destination; instead, it presented an opportunity for me to always grow and unfold. Learning is a way to keep focused, open to Spirit, and available to more wonderfulness than I can imagine. I also began to listen to great motivational and spiritual speakers like Les Brown, Jim Rohn, Tony Robbins, Zig Ziglar, Wayne Dyer, and Dr. Michael Bernard Beckwith, who I'm now studying under.

Jim Rohn once said, "Learn to work harder on yourself than you do on your job. If you work hard on your job, you'll make a living. When you work on yourself, you'll make a fortune." The part of that quote, "... when you work on yourself, you'll make a fortune!" is so true because it's putting the focus on what can be accomplished via the dreams, visions, and ideas that was given to you by Spirit. A fortune can be more than financial gain; it can also appear as freedom, peace, harmony, more time with family,

The Essential Pain and Peace of Life

reciprocal relationships, mentorship, and more. It's about taking the necessary steps to gain as much knowledge as possible to open to the greater possibilities that are seeking expression in your life.

I understood what I needed to do when the outline of *The Essential Peace of Life* was rejected. I had to let people know that I was there, and I had a message that needed to be shared. I could only accomplish this by working on myself and investing the time and energy into researching how to be a great inspirational speaker and author. In addition to reading books, I searched for trainings that would sharpen me as a speaker and author. I even became an Agape Spiritual Licensed Practitioner, not to just be a Spiritual Therapist, yet to have another way of working on myself and being an open and clear channel for Essence. My advice to you is to start creating your environment right now by finding out what you want out of life. What does that environment look like for you? Who are the people involved? What are the visions, dreams, and ideas that you have set aside? Once you've completed this self-inventory, begin to search out and invest in personal development tools that work for you. Have a since of urgency to fulfill those dreams, visions, and ideas. I printed and put up a poster size of my book cover in my work room so that I would be constantly reminded that I needed to finish this book and make sure you all receive this great information – information that will help reveal your greatness.

LIFE IS WHAT YOU MAKE IT

WHILE I WAS GOING THROUGH A DARK MOMENT IN MY life during my first marriage, I noticed I wasn't handling things very well. I had a very difficult time shaking what was going on at home and often took it to work with me. The pain that I allowed myself to endure during that time was at times unbearable and even had me catatonic. I allowed the story of what was taking place at that current time to have so much power, that I couldn't stop talking about in the form of complaining and whining. As you know, nobody wants to be around a whinner and complainer. While I was on my job answering phones for a banking company, I met a caller named Minister Elijah-Marie Reid out of Toronto, Canada. This was a very interesting call. We started talking about her bank account only for the conversation to shift to what was going on in my life. I was surprised yet I surrendered to what she was saying because I knew every word was for me. I knew True Essence was at work on my behalf. Minister Reid said, "... it is your responsibility to take responsibility of your wins by being the change you want to see. Remember, you cannot ask for change when you have not demonstrated authentic change and work on self." That was the first time I had ever heard how important it was that I changed myself from within to change my external environment. I was being given a gift through Minister Reid that would guide me in a different direction from how I was thinking and relating to what was happening in my life. Then she sent me a speech by Colin Powell, the first African American United States Secretary of State, titled *Bridging the Gap* and that was a gamechanger. I realized while reading that speech that it's important to know whom I'm associating with. I learned to be mindful of their actions and reactions of others and whether it aligned to my purpose in life. My mind was opened to a new understanding of what my environment should consist of and how I needed to look at the things going on in my life from that point on.

Months before my Uncle Joseph Peeler, my mother's brother, transitioned, he gave me instruction and different books to read. My uncle taught from the teachings of the Unity Church and new thought ageless wisdom, and he wanted to pass this knowledge to me. I was eager to receive this instruction because I was interested in being a minister and having my own spiritual center. I also sought wisdom that could help me navigate through the dark moment I was experiencing in my marriage. The one thing that stuck with me the most from those notes is that "God is All there is, Nothing Else." I was amazed at how powerful, and laser focused that statement and principle of truth was. It was a mandate to only focus on the Power and Presence that is never absent, is always with me, and is my everything – no matter what. My Uncle's notes continued, "There are no problems, situations or even issues in God. There is only God. There is only the one true power; everything else is an illusion." I had to allow those words to digest and take root in my being. At that moment, all I could see was the hurt, pain, and confusion of the dark time I was experiencing in my marriage. I'm glad that the seed was planted. I repeated that statement often to bring myself back into alignment with what was true about me. When I noticed my mood shifting because of an appearance of an issue or problem, I remembered my Uncle Joe's words, "God is all there is, nothing else." I would say that, and my focus went from how I could react to the situation to how I really wanted to feel in that moment. Instead of anger, fear, doubt or worry, I would focus on peace, love, joy, and harmony as my true nature.

Minister Elijah-Marie Reid and my Uncle Joe saw what Spirit was wanting to reveal and unfold as my life, and they knew that I needed to transform my mind for those changes to take place in my environment. If I stayed focused on what I thought I saw to be true, I would have never been able to see the possibilities of how things could be better. Over time I didn't focus on what was taking place with myself and my wife at the time and the pain it was causing, I started to focus on what I wanted to do with my life and to see what type of relationship I wanted to create on the outside, because it all depended on what type of relationship I had on the inside. I'm grateful for them both agreeing to be the vessels at that time of my life, a time when I was ready and willing to receive the guidance and direction, they had to give me.

SEEK YE FIRST

I AM AMUSED AT THE POWER I HAVE TO CREATE WHO I am in the eyes of others. I may not have a second chance to make a first impression, yet I do have a chance to change the impression I left the first time and make it a better one. If I wanted people in my life to be positive and upstanding, then I had to become positive and upstanding. Remember, what you focus on expands, and it is a universal law of life that will be fulfilled one way or another. Matthew 6:33 states, "Seek ye first the kingdom of God and all things will be added unto you." Or as my Uncle Joe said, "God is all there is, nothing else." When you seek within, you create the true environment that will manifest externally as your ideas, dreams, and visions. Allow your environment to be impressed by the greatness that you are and have within yourself. It is your rightful inheritance to gain the kingdom and everything within it. By not letting your current environment dictate and determine who you are and allowing the truth of who you are to be revealed in your life, you unfold into a greater you and your environment will follow suit.

4

BE HONEST WITH YOURSELF

∽

"To thine own self be true" is a line from the classic Shakespeare play *Hamlet* (Act I scene iii). Polonius speaks these words while giving advice to his son, Laertes, before he left for Paris. That one sentence was advice that Polonius wanted his son to embody. Spiritually, I believe this message was meant as a reminder to Laertes that he always knows what's best for him because of his connection with True Essence. When I allowed pain to have more of a definite part in my life, I didn't know how to really to be true to myself, because I wasn't trying to look at what was trying to be shown to me through those moments with it would arise. Each time I experienced pain in my life, that was the moment where I needed to take a look at what was wanting my attention to become more aware of my true self and allow peace to be my true nature. I now realize that I wasn't knowing who I really was. Because, when you know who you are and why you are here, you become unstoppable. You become aware of what you like and don't like and can stand tall when told differently. Your no means no, and your yes means yes. When you know the truth about who you are, you stand in it and are free because of it.

Being true to yourself allows you to respect yourself, which in turn allows you to have respect for others. I learned that I don't have the power to change other people; I can only change myself to create the outcome that is ultimately wanted and rightfully mine. This chapter discusses the importance of being true to Self and why it's important to maintain that focus despite what someone else says and the circumstances you might face. This chapter will also go into the "Three Muscles" that help you to know the truth about yourself, being comfortable with Self, and how feeling productive is important to feeling peace, which is the true nature of your being.

STRETCHING THE MUSCLES OF TRUTH

In high school, my gym teacher instructed the class on the importance of stretching before undertaking an activity. He said, "You can lie to me about how many stretches you've done and done properly, yet in the end you can't lie to yourself." I was young and didn't care what any adult said or thought of me. Like most of the students, I cheated on the proper number of warmups and paid for it in the end through muscle cramps and pulls. I didn't care about myself then, even when advised that I should. At that time, I didn't understand how important I was. By not listening, I risked pain and danced with possible injury.

"How many times has True Essence tried to talk to you directly or through others about being true to yourself?" I know I have missed the mark from time to time by not heeding the voice, which resulted in me experiencing hurt multiple times. I later realized that I wasn't doing what it took to be true or honest with myself, and I had to get on a regimen that would assist me in being true to myself. I discovered there are three muscles that need to be stretched to live optimally and as one's truest and best self: The listening muscle, the mental (learning) muscle, and the movement muscle.

In the beginning stages of *The Essential Peace of Life*, I didn't do the proper stretching exercises because I believed what someone else said about my divine idea. I was told that it wasn't going to be a suitable fit for the team and that I shouldn't waste my time pursuing it because no one would listen. I took what I knew to be true and tossed it aside like it was nothing. I didn't do the proper warmups to allow my idea to come into fruition, and experienced pain because I wasn't fulfilling my divine idea. I was in a constant battle with my inner thoughts and developed a negative attitude towards anyone who saw my potential because I didn't want to hear it. As much as I tried, I couldn't get away from my divine idea. It never left me. It continued to call out to me, and I had to do the work to make it happen.

The first muscle I began to stretch was my listening muscles, and I did this through meditation and prayer. I received guidance on what was needed to get the ball rolling. When I was still, quiet, and to myself, I'd write down everything I heard to decipher it later. Once I understood the messages received, I outlined the steps that I'd need to take. I began to practice the art of listening to the Presence daily. As I did, people would come into my life with directions and guidance that helped me with what I was creating, which was another way for me to hear from

Spirit. As I worked the listening muscle, my mental muscles began to strengthen as well. I invested in personal development classes, books, websites, and welcomed information from people that helped unfold the mindset needed to bring forth this vision. All was based on the directives I received during my quiet (and sometimes loud) time, which supplied me with the information that would help me practice and maintain a strong mental muscle.

Then, there are the movement muscles. In this area, you create a strategic plan of action to build the idea, vision, or dream then take the steps to bring it into fruition. It's alright to have an idea and vision, yet it's another thing to act on it. Movement is essential as it allows you to make the mistakes necessary to grow you and the idea. It also helps build momentum and allows for consistent unfoldment of the idea, vision, and dream.

Stretching is extremely important when exercising and playing sports and is equally important when fulfilling the ideas, vision, and dreams given to you by Spirit. There was something within me that required me to properly stretch my muscles and move on the dream that desired to express through me. I know this to be true for you also. Whether it is an invention, a non-profit organization, a small business, or music you want to create, whatever comes up for you is for you to do. When you follow that prompting, you will also find that this idea or vision is to assist in the development of others. I had to forego the untruths about me and begin to move in the truth of who I was. I no longer could ignore what was important to me. I had the ability to accomplish something great in my life and that needed my attention more than what anyone else thought of me and the beliefs I created to hinder myself.

Key Point: Only you know who you are despite what someone else may think they know about you. As the Chinese philosopher Lao Tzu said, "At the center of your being you know who you are, and you know what you want."

KNOW YOUR FEELINGS, KNOW YOURSELF

Whenever my stomach tightens up, I know that I must pay extra attention to my surroundings. You can say it's my Spidey sense kicking in. The tingling sensations can either be a warning or it can be an exciting, joyful, and happy feeling about something that hasn't revealed itself yet. No matter what, when I feel that sensation, I know that I'm being prepared to receive some information that would be beneficial to and for me. Yet growing up, it was very difficult to be able to move on what I am feeling and allow myself to have the safety I needed to flourish in my early life. Being hindered by someone that had some control over my life and how I was act and react to things, didn't allow me the freedom to be able to be fully in touch with myself and express what I feeling and know to be true for me to be and do in that moment. That's why this part is so important to me to express to you all, that your feelings are extremely important and that no matter what they must be felt, understood, and followed, to have the optimal outcome for your own life's unfoldment.

In Chapter 1, I shared the story of reconnecting with Mr. Aquillo after eight years and the sense of joy I felt in my gut when he mentioned the college program. That feeling prompted me to enroll in the program and now, I am a college graduate who creates music. Following that feeling of joy allowed me to be true to myself and was the impetus for me to unfold more into the creative being that I am.

There is also a peace of mind that comes when you trust the feelings that are coming up for you as these feelings always have information to give us. Many feelings that people deem bad such as anger, worry, doubt, frustration, and unworthiness surface when it is time to welcome and create a new belief system. These feelings arise as markers that there is an outdated illusion tied to your past that you must heal. There is a belief in place that no longer has a place in your life and it's time to release it. It's essential to D.I.G – go deeper in the groove – to acknowledge that those feelings are there. Those feelings matter and by acknowledging them, you create space for the truth of who you are and the power that you are to surface.

Having and understanding my feelings allows me to know who I am and what Spirit has in store for me. Aligning with my feelings affects how I create my life by helping me to either embrace what is helpful to fulfill my dreams or release what isn't in alignment for that fulfillment. Allowing myself to trust what I feel helps me to choose the direction I know is right for me, which comes by listening to the Source within. Your feelings are important and as long as you check in with Spirit about what you're feeling, then you won't be steered in the wrong direction.

LOSING WHO YOU THOUGHT YOU WERE

When I was around 12 years old, I used to wake up on the floor or in a chair after a black out. When I came to and saw my parents surrounding me, I would ask, "What is going on? Why are you looking so upset with me?" Their response would always be, "You know exactly what you did!" I didn't remember what happened and how I got to where I was. Trust me, I had no problem admitting if I did something wrong, yet in this case, I couldn't even tell a lie to get out of trouble if it came to that. To my knowledge, I was telling the truth and all I could do was sit there and pray someone or something could help me out of the situation. Things worsened for me. One morning, I woke up in the principal's office at school and saw my father standing next to me. Again, I didn't know how I got there and what took place. I was told that I stood up during class and told my teacher to shut up. I thought they were kidding because I really liked my teacher, Mrs. Delbello. I got expelled from that school, placed on punishment for months, and eventually placed in another school. On top of that, I was labeled again as a bad child.

The blackouts continued into my new school. I would wake up at my desk or in the principal's office, confused about what had happened. There were even times when I couldn't remember the work I was doing. No matter how hard I tried it was as if it wasn't enough in my classes and my grades suffered. I continued to be punished, was forced to have a tutor, and was treated like a child with serious behavior issues. It was all hard for me to understand and accept. I used to do well in school yet at that time, my grades didn't reflect who I remembered myself to be. The one thing that I never wanted was to disappoint anyone, especially my parents. I looked at old report cards and noticed that my grades were stellar prior to the blackouts. I wanted to have the grades that kept my parents happy with me and I earnestly searched for ways to make that happen. Even though I knew I was doing my best, I felt alone and untrustworthy. I felt everyone believed the narrative my parents told of me, which was that I was a bad child.

After a few months in the new school, I got a break. The principle noticed that I had a petit mal seizure while I was playing outside during gym. She saw me running when I suddenly stopped in my tracks before running again. She told my parents in a meeting that I had experienced an acute form of epilepsy and encouraged them to take me to the doctor for a check-up. She told them that it was serious and could be treated and assured them that I could even grow out of it. Finally, my blackouts had a prognosis.

I made it a point from that moment on to be true to myself and show who I really was. If I didn't know how to do something, I would find out how. No matter what someone thought of me based on the rumors they heard about me, I focused on the truth that I wanted to reflect in my life. I am doing all this while I haven't transmuted the pain from those events that took place before my parents came to terms with what was really happening with me. Yet, I was doing everything possible to be who Spirit wanted me to be and I still have stopped to this day. I knew that I wasn't at fault for what took place, even when I couldn't remember what was going on with me. I worked hard to be seen as a productive child and focused on improving my grades, which was all that mattered to me at that time.

As you can imagine, I developed a lot of beliefs about myself and my potential during the time of my undiagnosed blackouts. However, I believe that what happened to me was a way for me to be closer to Source. I had to learn how to trust the Essence within and choose to see the wonder that was in me. My communication became stronger, and I learned to trust my feelings. Although I would've loved to have the support and understanding of my family and close friends, I had started to develop a relationship with something deeper. In those blackout moments, I learned that freedom couldn't be given from an external source. Freedom first starts within. As time went on, I began to understand that my direction for living wasn't what my mother and father thought. There was already a plan in place for my life before I was even born. Since that is the truth of my being, only True Essence and I know what is best for me.

LEARN TO LOVE YOURSELF AND THE PAIN

In Chapter 3, I discussed the importance of boundaries as a way of self-love, and I want to emphasize now the importance of learning to love yourself. This is what I believe being true to you is about. If no one else ever tells you that they love you, then tell yourself "I love me." In the end, it's only you and the Great One. During my the pethora of times that I was enduring those seziures, I was told one to many times, some to my face and others by action, that I'm on my own and I have to go to God because I was given up on. I never thought that I would be living in a home with people that didn't want to do all they could to help there child through something that they had no way of getting through on their own. That's when I first noticed that I was left with my pain to go through this world to make the best of that I could with what I didn't know. Yes, I still had a roof over my head and food to eat, yet I didn't have the support to show the love that I wanted and deserved. I had to find ways to love myself and do it the best way I knew how and learned to trust Essence during my growth process. I realized that someone else didn't have to tell me they loved or enjoyed me; it's about me loving who I am, because I am love. Being in daily communion with True Essence allowed me to love myself daily and revealed my worthiness and greatness. I honor the love that I am by embracing the unique individual that I am. I had to give myself permission to be me and the courage to continue to do so.

Admittedly, this process of self-love and acceptance was not easy, especially during a time of my life when I felt isolated and misunderstood by almost everyone. I had to learn how to not replay in my mind the scenarios and things people said to me, which was a challenging feat. At one point, I began to ask others who I was because there was so much, I couldn't remember or retain. Their responses frustrated me, and I felt I was losing my mind even more. I felt like I lost time, respect, and what I believed was love of my parents and family. I was like a paralyzed person who was learning how to walk again, even though the memory of knowing how to walk before was still there. So much of my adolescence was spent on me having seizures, defending myself, and being ignored. I sought out help yet the more I did, I would be told that I already knew what to do. The more I heard those responses, the more I thought I wasn't productive enough. I figured that the way to be loved was to conform to what I was being told and not to what I understood. Each time I tried to conform; it didn't work. My conforming didn't make any difference in the other person, just me. My changing wasn't the truth of who I was and there was no joy in my life at all.

Rollo May, a distinguished psychologist and author of *Man's Search for Himself*, wrote, "The opposite of courage in our society is not cowardice, but conformity." At that time, I made the decision to listen to other's beliefs about me than what the Universe knew about me. I was willing to give up my courage to try to please someone who I would never be able to please no matter how hard I tried.

This lack of self-love spilled over into other areas of my life as well and played out at different points of my life. I experienced it the most when my ideas were rejected and belittled by management at the multi-level marketing company I worked for. I thought that if I couldn't define myself in the company division in Buffalo, New York, that I wouldn't be a success. I couldn't see another pathway to wealth at the time. Despite my better judgment, I stayed at the company when I knew to move on. Similarly, I experienced this when I asked someone very close to me to help me become a preacher. I was told that preaching was not for me and to consider pursuing a different role in the church. Because I tried so hard to meet other's standards of me, I turned away from and neglected the love that desired to express as me. I pushed aside what True Essence had in store for me. Luke 9:25 asks this question, "For what is a man/woman advantaged, if he/she gains the whole world, and loses his or herself, or be cast away?" Instead of loving myself and trusting that I'm productive enough to pursue my visions, dreams, and ideas, I relied on someone else's opinion and confirmation.

It was a process I had to undergo to see that I was wonderful and worthy of my love. I had to understand that when I love myself, I'm loving Spirit because I and Spirit are one. That was the only confirmation I needed to move forward with my life. When I acknowledged the greatness that I am, then I began to gain my courage back. I began to walk with the confidence that I'm everything that I'm supposed to be. When Source is pleased, I'm pleased and when I'm pleased, Source is pleased. I learned that what people thought about me was none of my business. Here is a suggestion: Listen only to the Source within and pay close attention to what Source has to say about you. That guidance will never lead you astray and will only guide you towards the path of self-love. The pain that I had within me was doing most of the driving because it was the very energy that keep me going to get wanting myself to feel and be loved by me. If I didn't have that drive I don't know where I would be today, yet I'm so glad I did and allowed myself to always want better and more for myself because I deserve it. Do everything possible to allow the greatness you are to shine, because it is your rightful inheritance and there is no greater love than self-love.

BE WHO YOU WERE CREATED TO BE

OSCAR WILDE, THE CONTROVERSIAL BRITISH AUTHOR of the late 19th century, said it best, "Be yourself; everyone else is already taken." Each person is uniquely made and has different gifts and talents. Each person also has unique ways of responding to a given situation. Individuality is to be celebrated, not manipulated, or controlled. Sadly, being oneself isn't always valued and I've noticed this the most in work environments. Conformity is valued over individuality and seen as a way to keep control. This also plays out in relationships where one person wants the other to act a certain way so that they feel comfortable. In the end, asking someone to be something that they are not never works out – for either party.

When I worked for a division of Citi Group, I was given the opportunity to lead a marketing group. I was given certain duties to perform and believed I had to change who I was and how I interacted with the group to gain the full extent of the promotion. I conformed and modeled my behavior after the person who gave me the position. I didn't think my kind, fun-loving, and thoughtful personality would be enough for the position. Instead, I became mean, stern, and distant. I though the staff would respect me in the same way they did the previous leader, yet it was just the opposite. The team members began to complain despite the numerous meetings I held to make them happy, and things only worsened. Despite the changes I was trying to make, I was removed from the position. Only then did I realize the value in being myself. I should have made the choice to create my own way for the program to run more effectively. Although it didn't turn out the way I thought it would, working at Citigroup proved to be a valuable learning experience for me. I learned that who I am is always enough.

The great thing about being yourself is that it fosters an environment of respect and mutuality. We are all One with the Universe, connected to the Divine Mind, yet unique in our giftedness and how we each are to express those gifts. I implore you to never let another person attempt to change you unless you have asked for help in bettering something about yourself. I believe that people should only enhance who a person is already. I call them visionaries because they can see greatness in a person and help to bring that excellence to the front.

I implore you to take the time to understand who you are and who you are meant to be. Take the time to discover what makes you feel phenomenal. Be open to the joy that you are and bring it with you to any and every situation. I guarantee you that there are so many talents and abilities within you that awaiting to be revealed. As you uncover more of you, you'll begin to enjoy more of you – and that's a feeling that you won't be able to live without.

BE YOUR CREATIVE SELF

When a feeling comes upon you to move forward on, move forward on it. There is a high probability that what you are feeling is the urge of your dreams, visions, and ideas that are seeking freedom through expression. There is a part of you that is beckoning to spring forth in new and exciting ways. It's very interesting when I'm around people who complain about their job repeatedly and don't believe they can do anything different. They feel they can't expand into other areas that would bring joy into their lives. They have bought into the belief that where they are is the only opportunity for them to be and grow. So much negative energy is spent on what can't be done, instead of directing that energy towards want can be done. Once there is an understanding that there is plenty of opportunity to acquire whatever anyone wants, there won't be any doubt about expanding outside of the comfort zone. The need to complain will turn into a need to share the joy of life.

I used to be one of those complaining types on the job, didn't like the way the boss talked and or treated me. It was as if there was specific way of being and treating people what someone becomes a manager or supervisor. It never made any sense to me what would ever make a person believe that one could get someone to do a great job on their job by instilling fear into them, instead of finding the persons strengths and creativity to make the most out of a persons working experience. I was always the one to try something different and make sure it was effective and efficient to show the supervisors to get there approval to continue in that manner. Sometimes it worked and other times either it didn't or some tweeks were made in order to make it seem like they came up with the idea. Either way I was being my creative self and finding a way to make my experience joy filled so that I would enjoy coming back to work.

    I never wanted to be in a position that I didn't enjoy, because I endured being that way living in a home where I couldn't be myself. Yet, I know one thing for sure is that if you want to continue to be your true creative self and continue to be the joy that you are, take the time to do what you love and make so that is the only thing that you do and build from there. Everything productive thing, idea, vision, and dream comes from the power that lives within you. That's why the very idea of The Essential Pain and Peace of Life kept coming back to me to do, because this is what I'm supposed to put out in the world and provide suggestions on how to live your life to the fullest by transforming pain into purpose. Just always be in the present moment whatever you put your mind to do and do it well.

When being true to Self is connected to doing what you love, everything becomes possible. Publisher and businessman Malcolm Forbes said, "The biggest mistake people make in life is not trying to make a living at doing what they most enjoy." If doing what you enjoy is what you strive for, then do what you must to make it so. I recommend exploring what you want to do, practicing it, mastering it, and making it completely yours. Believe me when I say that you can do it. I'm a living example and am experiencing the fruits of doing what I love. I marvel at the various ways that I get to be creative and am eager to see what else is waiting to unfold through and as me. I love what I do, and I love myself enough to have joy in doing what I want. And I know that this way of being and experiencing life is possible for you, too.

5

THE CONSCIOUS AND SUBCONSCIOUS MINDS ARE KEY

∼

I am a student of the mind, and it is one of my favorite subjects. I've spent a lot of time reading books on the conscious and subconscious minds, and I'm continuously fascinated at the power and potential each possess. The first book I read on the conscious and subconscious minds was *Psychogenesis: Everything Begins in Mind* by Jack Addington, and admittedly, much of what he wrote about made little sense to me. I didn't believe the techniques and concepts he shared in the book would work for me. For example, there is a section in the book that states that we will experience either positive or negative situations which stem from the narrative and beliefs held in the conscious and subconscious minds. It went on to say that we have the power to monitor and transform the thoughts that flow from and are imbedded in the mind. I didn't find it important while reading the book to completely change my thinking, speaking, and feeling just for life to work on my behalf. Yet I never put the book down and reread it numerous times and reference to this day. Then I met Rev. Michael Beckwith and listened to his teachings, and he was saying the same thing that I read in the book. He iterated that this is a feeling universe, we have the power within us to cultivate our lives, and that's where we must live from. It was incredible to believe that I could change everything about me just from changing my mind.

After copious study, I opened myself to greater depths of power that I didn't realize I had through understanding my conscious and subconscious minds. When I became aware of how to use the power of the mind and began to make it a part of my everyday experience, I had no choice than to pay attention to what I was saying, thinking, feeling and how I was synced with the Source within. This chapter is dedicated to sharing some key points and practices that will support you in accessing the infinite power that resides in the conscious and subconscious minds. This chapter will touch on: 1.)

The importance of the conscious and subconscious minds, their functions, and how to use them; 2.) How True Essence within is one with and works with the subconscious and conscious minds; and 3.) Ways to co-create with the power within by using both minds. 4.) How accessing the pain in both the subconscious and conscious minds can assist with the revealing and releasing process.

MY FOUNDATION OF UNDERSTANDING

A QUICK DISCLAIMER, WHEN I SPEAK ABOUT THE ONE Mind, I'm not talking in the human sense were the mind is associated with the brain. In this context I'm speaking of the Universal Mind the source of all that there is, that is the very power of life itself that I believe we all work through and as each of us.

There are two parts of the mind that work together to create and cultivate our dreams, visions, and ideas – the subconscious and conscious minds. The conscious mind is the action part, and the subconscious mind is the part that stores information. Both are activated through our thoughts, feelings, and the words we use daily. When we become aware of how they both work, we open ourselves to how powerful our words, feelings, and thoughts truly are. In truth, there is no way to elude what is created through the conscious and subconscious minds. The liberating thing is that there is always a way to reprogram and recreate any and everything – even our beliefs – through the power of the mind. There is indeed only One Mind and that is the Unlimited Spirit, yet this is the breakdown of the workings of the One Mind.

One of the sacred books of the Buddhist canon, *The Dhammapada* (Chapter 1, Verse 2), describes the importance of the mind in this way, "All things are preceded by the mind, led by the mind, created by the mind. If somebody speaks or acts with a purified mind, hence happiness follows him like a never departing shadow." The mind is a powerful asset and can take you wherever you want to go and create whatever you want to create. If joy is to be expressed, we have the power of the mind to become aware of the joy that is already within. If there is a vision or idea of a better home, job, or even creating a business, the power of the mind will work to create just that. And this only works when the thoughts, words, and feelings are synchronized with consciousness.

CONSCIOUS MIND

THE CONSCIOUS MIND IS THE MOST POWERFUL PART OF the mind and holds all the thoughts a person has and had in the past. It's the communication and action part of the mind. The word *conscious* means "being aware of one's own existence, sensations, thoughts, and internal knowledge." The conscious mind is where thoughts (seeds) are formed, and it is responsible for every decision made. As Proverb 23:7 states, "As a man/woman thinks in his/her heart, so is he/she" and this is true for what is thought in the conscious mind. Whatever you continuously think on will form in the material realm. I kept my mind on not being a bad boy for a very long time. I held on to that idea thinking I was moving forward believing I was making a difference, where I was still seeing me as a bad boy, instead of a great and wonderful being. There is no way around it, nor will it be denied. I began to realize that what I thought, felt, and spoke about on a consistent basis led to the outcomes I experienced in my life. What I desired didn't manifest because I was focused on what I didn't want. It's interesting because that whole time I was wasting energy and spending time on the inconsequential and didn't even notice it.

FEELING AS THE MIND

THE CONSCIOUS MIND IS ALSO AFFECTED BY OUR feelings and emotions. Before the thought is thought and the word is spoken, there is a feeling that is created. There are many definitions of the word *feel*, yet I'm going to just mention a few to help the point of this section. Feel means "to have a sensation of (something), other than by sight, hearing, taste, or smell; to be or become conscious of; to be emotionally affected by; to have a particular sensation or impression of." A feeling can be anger, sadness, fear, happiness, passion, excitement, joy, love, and the like. Any mood shift created in the body that causes a tingling and attitude sensation is a feeling.

A feeling acted upon in love, joy, and peace will create thoughts of its kind. Alternatively, a feeling of anger, sadness, angst, and depression will create thoughts and experiences of its kind. It's imperative to be mindful of any feelings that will not create the desired outcome. You can do this through the D.I.G method discussed in Chapter 2. Simply take a moment to feel into what you're feeling and after gathering the necessary information, consciously shift how you're feeling. Let's revisit a story I've shared in earlier chapters where I allowed someone else's opinion to hinder me from building a business. The feelings I had at the time was worry, less than, and doubt. Those feelings created thoughts that were counter to what I really wanted, which was to be successful. I felt unsuccessful and like I had to prove myself to another when the only person I had to prove anything to was myself. Also, the feeling of pain that I had from the experience with my parents when it pertains to the illness I once had. Those feelings of abandonment, loneliness, and unloved, really had effect on me, when all I wanted to feel was loved, belonged, and wanted. I had already put what wasn't true in motion and I didn't do anything about it to make myself feel otherwise. I understand and now know that my feelings create the very thoughts that I focus on or not. In either case, I have the choice. I have the choice to catch the feeling before it becomes a thought that I don't want to eventually experience. I have the choice to shift it from something that feels negative to something more aligned to what I desire to feel, such as joy, love, peace, and harmony. This shift in feeling will shift my thoughts and will be expressed as my new attitude.

THINKING AS THE MIND

When I was a part of the multi-level marketing team, there was a time when I truly enjoyed what I was doing. After a while, I began to wonder why I wasn't gaining the type of success that I saw other people enjoying. I wanted to build a large team and earn substantial amounts of money, yet it wasn't working out that way for me. In hindsight, I realize that the thoughts I focused on, thoughts of worry, lack, and fear, kept me from experiencing success in the way I desired.

I look at my experience with my parents and how I looked at what was happening to me will they were moving past what was going on with me after they got the diagnosis and I was still stuck at being that little child that believe he was a bad child, holding the firm the pain in endured while my parents didn't believe me. It was that moment that created the thoughts that I had about what was true and what I believed other people believed. With that I have created thoughts that, people wouldn't like me for me, I must do what it takes to make people believe I'm a wonderful person, and I must prove that I deserve anything productive to happen in my life.

My thoughts at that time were all about what I didn't want instead of what I did. I thought I was developing thick skin against the negative words directed towards my personal life and business production, yet I was attracting more of what I didn't want because I believed what was said to me and about me. I rejected the productivity that was trying to develop in my life and business. Not once did I realize that to change the situation, I had to change my focus and thoughts, which in turn would have reflected in my team size, the amount of money everyone on the team earned, and also how I saw myself so that I believe that other people would see my trues self just like I would.

Even though I was part of a team, and I looked up to my upline, the responsibility of success was mine. Same with the relationship with my parents and other people that I have encountered throughout my life. It's my responsibility to respond to life in the way that it was going to benefit me and create the outcome that I truly desired for my life. I later learned that to receive what is rightfully mine that my thoughts must be focused on the best, greatest, and marvelous expression of my unique life. This is done by affirming moment by moment the desired dreams, ideas, and visions that have been given to me by Essence. I must know without restraint that what I desire is possible for me. I wish I would've had this knowledge when I was a young boy and part of the multi-level marketing team, yet I am grateful for the understanding I now have. I can only imagine how powerful it would've been to switch my thoughts and feelings to create and attract what I truly wanted. There is no better time than the present, and now I have the wisdom that will help me gain my inherited manifestations.

SPEAKING AS THE MIND

WORDS ARE POWERFUL. DEPENDING ON HOW THEY ARE used and spoken, they create a feeling that is felt by the speaker and the receiver. This can create great or not-so-great outcomes. How do words work with the conscious mind? The words spoken reaffirm the thoughts that someone might have, which creates a belief that later creates that person's environment. Proverbs 18:21 of the Amplified Bible says, "Death and Life are in the power of the tongue, and those who love it and indulge it will eat its fruit and bear the consequences of their words." This scripture applied to me at several points in my life. I think about my relationship with my parents and how angry I was at how they treated me when I was experiencing seizures. I was a very hurt person and I spoke a lot about what I didn't like about them. I spoke so much that I wasn't open and available to what Spirit was trying to do for me in my life at that time. This negative talk trickled into the intimate relationships I had with the women in my life because I was trying to get from them what I thought I didn't get from the relationship with my mother. I was unable to heal from the pain I experienced in my youth and hindered the relationship with my mother from becoming one of respect and love. I didn't love myself because I still believed that I wasn't loved and or loveable, and I spoke to whoever would listen to my complaints. I created – through my conscious mind – the ideal environment to support the words that I spoke about my mother which manifested the women that I attracted in my life.

Words are extremely powerful. They create beliefs that will rent space in your mind and if repeated, will create the intended environment. It's imperative to mind your feelings and thoughts as they form the foundation for the words you speak. Those words not only harm you, yet they also bring harm to the people you speak the words to.

STAY TUNED IN

IN HIS BOOK *MAKING THE CONTACT*, AUTHOR ROBERT Russell mentioned about having the perfect consciousness of goodness and how Jesus maintained it. "He was aware every instant of the transforming power within him upon whom he could call at any time for anything he needed. The goodness within was a living reality permeating his whole being and radiating from him as a tremendous, quickening power." When focused, anyone can access that same transforming and radiating power of the conscious mind and develop wondrous things. The conscious mind holds internal knowledge, and it is where the power and ability to create begins.

When I think of the conscious mind holding internal knowledge, I am reminded of several times when I fixed certain items without an instruction manual. As I allowed the power within to guide me, I fixed whatever was broken and even made it better than before. In my early teen years, my family owned a pair of stereo speakers that no longer worked. I had a deep feeling that I could get those speakers to work again. I received a download on what needed to be done to get the speakers functioning again. I listened with faith and followed the guidance I received. I opened the back of one of the speakers to see how the wires were connected. At the end of the V-shaped wire that connected to the speaker, one side had a plug while the other side was broken. I cut the broken plug off, stripped the insulation back, and secured the metal part of the wire. I completed the project by placing black electrical tape around the exposed part of the wire. I plugged the speaker into the stereo system and the speaker produced beautiful, high-quality sounding music. I didn't have any training in repairing electronics and since then, I have fixed other stereo speakers, ultimately creating a surround sound system in my room.

From that moment on, I allowed myself to try my hands at other projects and trusted that everything would be done to wondrous perfection. I trusted that I would have nothing to lose, yet a lot of knowledge to gain. When I heard the instructions from within on how to repair the sound to the speakers, I followed them and allowed the outcome to work through me. A passage from *Psychogenesis: Everything Begins in Mind* by Jack Addington is appropriate here, "... man can do whatever he is able to conceive in his mind, receive in his consciousness, expect with assurance and accept in actual experience." I believe this is how inventions are created, melodies are composed, and clothes are designed – through conceiving in one's mind and receiving in consciousness the very idea of what's to be created. Consider these questions: *What are you leaving behind as a thought that could enhance your life and the life of others? Are you allowing the illusion of fear to evade whatever you vision not to work?* If so, it's time to move past that way of thinking and give in to your inner power – the conscious mind – and allow the internal knowledge to work on your behalf. You have everything it takes to unfold great things in your life. It's happening for me every time I make myself available, and it can and will happen for you if you allow it.

My Uncle Frank, my fathers' brother, is wonderful at remodeling homes, painting (both homes and art), and doing collision work on cars and trains. I saw him in action many times and the work he did was always excellently done. He transformed the shelves and the refrigerator doors in my grandparent's kitchen. I even had a chance to work with him at his home in New Jersey when he added a new floor. He taught me how to develop a frame to create a walk-in closet and how to drop a ceiling. He explained to me that one day he simply made the choice to remodel and repaint the kitchen and ceiling at my grandparent's house, with little to no experience beforehand. He decided to learn how to do carpentry work and has expanded into other areas of remodeling and repair. I wish I had pictures of his handiwork to show you how the

Universe was at work within and through him. To know that he is now working for the railroad in the collision shop just shows that he has expanded his abilities through his conscious mind. I believe that everyone has that same ability. It's possible and time to tap in.

Here is an exercise I'd like for you to try. This practice can help you let go and allow the conscious mind to assist in anything that you desire and have a vision to manifest. Take something that you've always wanted to do and place it in your mind's eye. Sit in silence and bring your awareness to the idea. While focusing on what is desired, begin to listen for direction. Take this quiet moment to hear what is required to begin the co-creating process. Listen to the voice within, the voice that you know won't lead you astray. Notice how what is being said reflects your creative nature and shows how possible it is to expand your abilities and accomplish the very thing desired.

Remember the song I mentioned in Chapter 1 that my cousin wrote, "Becoming what you already are?" Here is another part to focus on, "Celebrate, because the answer is within you!" Anytime your awareness is open to say yes, the answers are revealed that enhance the ideas and visions you hold. Equally important as receiving the enhanced wisdom is to celebrate what is coming through. That feeling of joy, when it takes over your entire body, sets a feeling tone that allows whatever you desire to come to you quicker. Allow the joy to flood your existence. It is time to get what is rightfully yours.

I am reminded of a line from the 1985 classic movie, *The Last Dragon*. "This is when the spirit takes over mind and guides the body without thought." The Last Dragon is about a young, talented martial arts expert in search of a higher power, yet he was looking for this power outside himself. He later realized that the very power he was looking for was already within him. His teacher reminded him that, "There is one place that you have not yet looked, and it is there that you will find the master." He had everything within him to obtain the power and knowledge that he sought after. It's the same for you. When you begin to trust your first thought, you send a signal out to your conscious mind that you trust the knower who knows, which is your very life. Follow that first thought and see the greatness that it will bring forth. Imagine and marvel at the wonder that it could bring to you. You will be amazed at what can come from your time of concentration and meditation.

When I was 16 years old, my father assigned homework to the Bible Study class he taught, which was to read Chapter 1 from the book of James. The homework for the following week was to come back with an understanding and explanation of what we read. As I read that chapter, verses 5-8 stood out to me and led me to other connecting verses. I started to develop a sermon and the words flowed through. I was in the zone and was very grateful when I was chosen to share my homework in class the next week. That same message became my trial sermon, which later developed a hunger within me to become a speaker. Fast forward to my first year in college, I had the opportunity to speak for my friend's father's church conference in Rochester, New York. That was my first revival ever and a wonderful experience that lasted forever in my heart and mind. I was bit by the speaking bug, and eager for more speaking opportunities.

My conscious mind allowed me to understand what I was reading and how to make it plain and simple for others to understand. That exercise also inspired me to take public speaking classes, which led to me becoming an inspirational speaker. Yes, I was worried about what people would think about the message, yet that didn't matter because it felt awesom to me and that's all that mattered. I followed the information and instructions that were developing within me and got a glimpse of the greater things I would accomplish. It all was preparing me for this moment, where I get to be a blessing through my gifts.

The conscious mind is a very powerful part of the mind that opens you to endless and attainable possibilities. It all starts with you listening and saying yes to the guidance you're receiving. Through listening, you unfold the greatness that you already possess, which leads you to discovering who you really are and what is already within you to become.

WHAT IS THE SUBCONSCIOUS MIND

THE SUBCONSCIOUS MIND MEANS, "OPERATING IN THE mind beneath or beyond consciousness, the totality of mental processes of which the individual is not aware; the storage facility for all thoughts." You can liken the subconscious mind to the part of the glacier that is underwater – unseen yet always present. In his book, *The Strangest Secret*, Earl Nightingale writes, "The mind is like soil; no matter what you plant it will come forth." The subconscious mind is where our ideas, dreams, negative and positive thoughts, and beliefs reside. Seeds are planted and take root in the subconscious mind and depending on their kind, will either produce a positive or negative experience. It's amazing to me how much of my young and adolescent life I have spent being directed by the thoughts, beliefs, and actions of my subconscious. A lot of my pain was expressed through most of my actions and the reactions that I have presented before the world has not been of those that allow me to show that I am a productive person. And I have found the way that most people treat is based on what I believe that is what is buried within, being expressed in conversation, as a revelation to me of that which needs to be transformed to reveal my true nature. Through the process of D.I.G (Deeper in the Groove), you can weed out any beliefs and ideas that are held within the subconscious.

Although the analogy of a glacier is a great one to work with when describing the subconscious, I'd like us to consider Nightingale's soil analogy. The seeds are the ideas, thoughts, and beliefs that are planted within the soil (subconscious mind). The nurturing plants are the encoded and destined ideals given to you by Source. The weeds are ideas, thoughts, and beliefs that were planted in the mind by other people and external circumstances. The subconscious mind works intimately with the conscious mind. As the seeds grow from the subconscious mind, they manifest of their kind into the conscious mind, which projects it into your lived experience. As mentioned previously, the conscious mind is the action part of the mind, and the subconscious mind is the storage of all the thoughts and ideas to be acted upon. Cornelia and Jack Addington, in a life-transforming book titled, *The Perfect Power Within*, says, "The subconscious side of the mind follows the orders of the conscious mind... It will never question the orders or directions given it by the conscious mind and has the ability to follow through unerringly in carrying out these orders." This is very powerful because the subconscious mind holds every thought, belief, and idea that was either given or self-planted. Whatever is focused on will create an outcome whether it's wanted or not. This leaves everything in your power to notice and maintain what is you and to be more mindful of what you feel, think, and speak. Yes, being aware of your feelings, thoughts, and speech plays a role with the subconscious mind, too. This reminds me of the Proverbs 4:23 that says, "Guard your heart above all else, for it determines the course of your life." Although we are talking about the two parts of the mind, remember that feeling is what creates your thoughts, and feeling is associated with the heart. It can be said that the heart and mind work together to create what is wanted or not wanted. To guard your heart (or mind) is to carefully watch what's being planted either from yourself or someone else and cultivating what has been planted to produce the feeling and environment that is desired.

POST PLANTING

THE IDEA THAT THINGS JUST POP UP RANDOMLY IS MOOT when looking at the subconscious mind. You can say what's really happening in those moments is that a suppressed thought, belief, and idea has come to the surface to be revealed. Because of this, I believe that the True Self is always finding a way to reveal its nature – the divine plan that was planted long before outside ideas, beliefs, and plans took root – in an individual. Even if a person experienced a time of misdirection, it is still possible to course correct and that's where the subconscious comes in. I believe the subconscious already has and knows everything that is needed to have the perfect life. Since a person's environment isn't who they are, it is possible for them to live a life of joy, peace, love, and harmony. Just like it is imperative that you are aware of the active thoughts in the conscious mind, it is equally important to be aware of the hidden thoughts that are held in the subconscious and choosing whether to allow them to grow or release them.

While discovering information on the subconscious, I was fascinated to learn how much information is planted there from the opinions and ideas of other people. When I would have an epileptic episode, ideas about who I was, and my behavior were planted subconsciously by my parents and other family members that I didn't agree to. At the time, I didn't know what was going on or happening to me. There was so much taking place in a short period of time that I didn't know which way was up or down, what was true or false, what was real or an illusion. As a result, I cultivated a belief of unworthiness and attributed this to how my parents and others saw and felt about me.

From my understanding, a lot of people grew up with ideas, thoughts, and beliefs that were planted in their minds by other people such as parents, other adults, and friends. Those outside beliefs, if not monitored, could lead to an individual not fulfilling on the destiny that was encoded in them before conception. Some of those planted beliefs could be: No one can be successful as a business owner; You must only work a 9-5; If you want to paint you will become a starving artist; You can't make any money being a writer; and God is vindictive, to name a few. When such beliefs take hold, they can prevent the truth about a person from surfacing and being embraced. Instead of seeing this truth as their pure nature, the individual will see it as an impossibility. If not careful, those planted ideas can suffocate and stifle that person's true destiny.

THE SEEDS I PLANTED

IT'S IMPORTANT THAT YOU MIND THE WORDS YOU SPEAK into the universe. Words, just like our thoughts, can come back to surprise us in the forms of manifestations that may not be wanted. (I know that I shouldn't call anything in the Universe unexpected, because what I perceive as unexpected was really something that was dormant in the subconscious.) Many times, I have said things, positively or negatively, that happened. For instance, I used to wake up early in the morning and would bemoan the day. I'd say out loud, "I'm going to have a bad day." Sure enough, as I went through my day, nothing went right. The very thing I stated and focused on became my experience.

I love spades and I consider myself a decent player. I would trash talk during the game and when it was my turn to play, I would lose. The irony is that I had a winning streak going before the trash talk. Once I realized this pattern, I put trash talking to the side and concentrated on my hand. I began to win more games. Now don't get me wrong, I still do like to antagonize the other team, yet I've limited the amount of taunting I do so that I don't forfeit my spot in the game. Even something as trivial as trash talking is the subconscious mind at work. In both cases, my thoughts and beliefs created the outcomes I experienced.

My father used to remind me all the time to "think before you speak. What is being said causes a ripple effect on not just you, yet also the people around you." Words are seeds that are planted into the Universal Mind, later to be made manifest in the natural world. Despite the popular saying, words can – and often do – hurt. They influence our lives daily, yet it is up to us to choose how those words affect us. We can shift how we use our words through affirmations. An *affirmation* is the action or process of affirming something. It is, "being affirmed, emotional support or encouragement." Saying affirmations allows me to keep my mind focused on the wonder that is destined to happen in my life and to stay positive when my environment may want me to think otherwise.

Affirmations communicate in present tense the wonderful and positive statements that reveal your true nature. An example of an affirmation would be, "My life as the life of Spirit is always a shining example of the greatness that is within, through, and as me." This affirmation provides a new seed thought that is then planted in the subconscious mind, thus yielding a new belief for you to live from.

Remember Marianne Williamson's poem "Our Deepest Fear," mentioned in Chapter 2? In the poem, Williamson reminds us that we "are powerful beyond measure." And our power is found in our words. The power of our words and thoughts creates our respective worlds, which affects the world at large. When I began to pay attention to my external environment, I had to take inventory to find out the kind of seeds that I planted that contributed to what I was seeing. Taking inventory means remembering the thoughts and beliefs that you allowed yourself to focus on and making a choice to change them. You can switch a negative thought to a positive one immediately. You always have the option to change your thoughts. You always have the choice to reset your mental garden to produce the things you desire in your life. It is a practice and a worthwhile investment that guarantees exponential growth. I believe we all possess the ability to turn over the fallow ground of our subconscious mind so that new and great things can be created.

SEEDS OF THE REAL ME

DESPITE WHAT I THOUGHT OTHERS BELIEVED ABOUT ME, there was always something within me that desired for my true nature to be revealed. The real me desired expression. The real me desired to be noticed for who I truly was and not how someone else perceived me. This process of clearing the weeds was for me than anyone else. What looked like acting out was an opportunity for me to release the thought patterns that were planted by others about me. It was a chance for me to see my capabilities and to trust in True Essence. There was an internal transformation taking place and I was learning to trust that I was OK and my purpose in life had nothing to do with what people believed about me during my epileptic spells. What mattered most was how I chose to live, think, and believe about myself.

When I began to understand who I really was and the divine direction my life was going, I began to *D.I.G.* into my subconscious mind. This allowed me to create space for more productive thoughts so that my conversations and actions would display the joy I desired to manifest and express in my life. I found it important to explore my true Self and fulfill what was already in my Divine blueprint. I know that individuals meant well, and I did learn a lot during that time of my life, yet when I reconnected to what I was called to do, there was a new and exciting world to experience and enjoy. Once I experienced this newness, I made every effort to put myself in a position – through my thoughts, words, and feelings – to my life.

Let's revisit the example of me reading the Bible verse during Bible Study. As I was reading, I asked myself how I might deliver a message that would be understood and received by the congregation. That very question was placed in the subconscious mind. Again, the subconscious is the *soil* of the mind in which ideals are planted and later expressed into daily actions and responses. The mind, like any garden of flowers or vegetables, needs to be cultivated. All things that grow must be cultivated, watered, and placed where it can receive proper sunlight. The sunlight and watering process for the mind is our focus and our ability to say yes to the directions that our given by our consciousness. The answer to my question began to appear mentally in the form of examples. The answers surfaced to the conscious mind and action was taken. I had a clear picture of how to convey the revelation I had to the people. Because of that, I had a great experience that led to my first trial sermon.

ANOTHER FUNCTION OF THE SUBCONSCIOUS

OUR SUBCONSCIOUS MIND IS THE BREEDING GROUND FOR all our thoughts and beliefs. And, there is more. In his book *Psychogenesis,* Jack Addington explains the subconscious as, "the soil where the thoughts or directions from the consciousness are being cultivated to be made manifest. It is the dormant part of the universe where, when you're sleeping, it's working." After reading that, I felt the subconscious mind was even more powerful than the conscious mind because of what it also controls in the body. Whether I'm sleep or awake and without my help, the subconscious is assisting in the functioning of every organ. With no thought on my part, the digestive system breaks down the food or liquid I ingested. My heart pumps blood though my body, transferring different cells, antibodies, and other helpful organisms to help keep the body warm and energized. The respiratory system keeps oxygen flowing in and releases carbon dioxide, which aids the growth of plants and trees on this Earth. The nervous system – the center of all feeling, movement, seeing, and speaking – works properly to ensure I have an excellent quality of life. These are all examples of the subconscious mind at work helping me to fulfill my destiny. I'm amazed at how this body is working at a pace that I wasn't totally conscious of until I took the time to recognize and feel what my body was doing and how it's functioning. I have the option to control and move this body by my thoughts, which means I also have the power to heal myself by my thoughts and the words I affirm.

6

CO-CREATE THE LIFE YOU DESERVE

∽

Did you know that you are co-creating your life and all its experiences with the True Essence? Being a co-creator with True Essence is like being a co-signer for a loan or another type of negotiable contract or promissory note and you are equally responsible for what happens. When there is an agreement with the dreams, visions, and ideas within you, then when you say YES, you are agreeing to the greatness that is ready to come forth.

Growing up I said, "YES," to a lot of things that I had co-created throughout my young life. I allowed a lot to happen because of the pain that I didn't know how to transmute into productive energy. Most of my time was spent being what I believed the type of person my parents could be proud of and at the same time there were other ideas, visions, and dreams I was having that wasn't in alignment with what my parents wanted. So, I began to notice that even through my pain and hurt, Essence was still reaching out to me showing me so much that I could co-create with my life. It's interesting that even though I wasn't acting "right," reacting to things that caused problems, and may have had me looked at as some type of misfit, I was still being called to do wonderful and marvelous things with my life. Now all I needed to do was to be focused and be open to the direction that was being given to manifest the co-creations.

What does co-creator mean? Let's start with the second part of the word. Creator means, "a person that creates; to cause into being, to unfold from one's own thought or imagination." The prefix *co-* means an auxiliary or a person that gives aid of any kind, a helper. It also means jointness, united, to be together, not separate from and combined. By definition, a co-creator is one who assists in the act of creating. This gives the perfect understanding of your relationship with True Essence or Creator. You are an integral part in manifesting wondrous things.

As you probably figured by now, True Essence is the name I have given the power that lives through and as you and me. True Essence works as the conscious mind and gives us the directions to accomplish all ideas, dreams, and visions. Jesus the Christ was the supreme example of what it looks like to live on Earth and still be in relationship with True Essence. Jesus said, "I and my Father are one." (John 10:30). He understood his relationship with Source and how important it was to be a co-creator with Source. Jesus continually mentioned his relationship with God and how he received directions from True Essence. "Verily, verily, I say unto you, the Son can do nothing of himself, yet what he sees the Father do: for what things so ever he doeth, these also doeth the Son likewise." (John 5:19). When I began to understand this premise, I started to move with bigger faith in my dreams because I realized that the power within me wanted it these dreams just as much as I did and more. Despite what I did yesterday, last year, or 5, 10 years ago, I am still chosen to do co-create the type of life I have been shown to create with Essence. I have been forgiven even though no one else has and that's ok because Essence has the last and final say. Because of that, all I can do is do what it takes to get myself in aliment, open and available to what directions I'm being given. I began to trust that this power would assist in making any and everything possible for that dream to manifest.

MAKING THE AGREEMENT

Everything that could ever be imagined, envisioned, and thought of comes from within and we unfold it all through our willing YES. When we say yes and move by faith on the ideas True Essence has prepared for us, we are making a conscious agreement that all is well right now and everything has worked out for us to fulfill on those dreams. From writing, singing, and performing my own music, to speaking to millions of people and helping them expand their lives, to any other dream held in the mind, I am allowing myself to flow in the direction of my destiny, which is life that has already been created by True Essence. I have co-signed with the Source by saying YES.

Agreement means, "the state of being in accord; an arrangement that is accepted by all parties to a transaction; unanimity of opinion; and harmony in feeling." I like the last part of the definition *harmony in feeling*. When I make an agreement, I am saying, "YES" to what is coming up for me to accomplish and unfold. It's an understanding that gives me a feeling of harmony and peace because it's in alignment with the ideas, dreams, and visions that have originated from the Source within. I have noticed that when I agree to things that are not in the divine plans that have been prepared for me that I experience frustration and unease. It doesn't feel harmonious or peaceful and is quite forced and unaligned. I know the feeling I want, and that feeling is to always be peace. That happens by working through the pain of the past which will allow me to be open to the productiveness that's within me. I know that I'm not in alignment when I hear, feel, and know to go into a particular direction and choose to go in another. If I'm feeling something other than harmony and peace, then I know that I'm not in alignment. I know that it's important to follow what I hear and have faith that it is for the purpose of my evolution.

In Chapter 5, I mentioned that the subconscious stores and produces your thoughts and beliefs for the conscious mind to act on. It also gives directions based on the programmed ideals planted by Source, which is the starting process for co-creating. I realized I received various instructions daily on my dreams. These instructions or thoughts guided me to fulfill on what I said that I would complete. Every directive given from that point to unfoldment is the subconscious honoring the agreement. A lot of times, I would hear to go and move a certain way and I hesitated because I didn't feel it, or it didn't look like it was the right thing to do. When I went my own way, I'd usually end up saying after, "I could have gone with my first mind." I didn't trust the directions given that came with making the agreement. Have you ever had this happen to you? When you realized that you could have done exactly what you heard from within and didn't do it? The great thing to know is that there is always another chance to fulfill the agreement as the co-creator. There is no such thing as "one and done," "three strikes you're out" with the Universe. True Essence will never give away the very idea that is uniquely for you.

How did I know when something was meant for me? Easy: I knew from the visions and ideas that constantly stayed on my mind. I saw clearly what it could look like. The ideas sparked a deep sense of joy in me. I felt alive and possible. Whenever I thought of my dreams, visions, and ideas, I smiled like a man who was deeply in love. I had goose bumps all over me, all because of the joy I felt about them and that I could do something more with my life. I believe that when there is a feeling of continuous joy and excitement during the co-creating process, there is a knowing and feeling that everything is alright and is already done. I produce the very feeling of joy that is my nature and envision myself at a higher vibration than how I experienced life before.

The Essential Pain and Peace of Life

A POSITIVE MIND CO-CREATES ANYTHING

POSITIVE THINKING PLAYS A HUGE PART IN THE CO-creating process. It aligns with the law of attraction, which in brief is, "whatever we think about becomes our reality." Maintaining a positive mindset helps us to draw to us what we desire. Negative thoughts will surface every now and again, and that's normal. It's normal because when they arise it's time to see what pain is showing forth in the moment to be transmuted and harnessed for the appointed outcome. Positive thinking allows us to shift our focus to what we desire to happen as opposed to what we don't. Whether we think positively or negatively, the key point to remember is that it is our choice.

When I enrolled in the Music Business Program after being out of college for years, I came up against quite a few negative thoughts. I hadn't been in school for five years and was out of practice with the work I'd be required to do. On top of that, I had to take an entrance exam to even get into the program. At the time, I doubted if I'd pass the exam and started to feel that I wouldn't get accepted. I had given up before I even tried to get started. I even told my girlfriend at the time, "I guess I'm going to have to take a loss on this one." And I meant what I said. I had the wrong mindset going into taking the exams.

Although my girlfriend encouraged me, I also had to remember why I was taking those exams and what my main goal was. I had a dream that I wanted to fulfill. There was something that I wanted to learn and become knowledgeable on and that was music. To do that, I had to pass the entry exam. I had moments that I didn't feel worthy of such a give to have the opportunity to go back to school to do something that I really wanted to learn. I had to first realize that I was someone of importance and value. I also realized that I had to change my mind set before entering the room to take my entry exams. I shifted my thoughts from "I'm not going to make it," to "No matter what, everything is working for my Success and I'm worthy, which is my true nature." I kept my focus on the task at hand. No matter what it took, I was going to learn and earn the degree that came with intensive study. Surprisingly, after shifting my thoughts, I passed the exam and went on to perform well in all classes. I earned my degree with high honors and made the dean's list for three consecutive semesters. I now own recording equipment, a guitar and keyboard, and I have written and recorded hundreds of songs. This is what happens when you transform your thinking to one that serves you and the desired outcome you want to experience.

NEW WINE FOR NEW WINE SKIN

I DIDN'T HAVE ANY REAL TRAINING ON HOW TO PUT something like The Essential Peace of Life program together. I was taught that the only way to make money was to work a regular job, not follow your dreams, visions, and ideas. Initially, I didn't think the program was possible. I didn't think anyone would listen and be transformed by the message because my upline didn't think it would work. Sadly, at that time, I had more faith in what my upline had to say than the very idea and vision of The Essential Peace of Life program given to me by True Essence. A lot of that came from me believing that people knew what was better for me to do with my life opposed Power and Presence within that is my life and only wants the best for me.

The old wine skin, or environment, that I created from those old mindsets no longer served me as something new and exciting was trying to be created from within. Despite how long it would take, those ideas, dreams, and visions were not going to leave until I moved forward on them. I realized that to step fully in being the co-creator that I was destined to be that I couldn't place new wine in old wine skins. Said differently, I couldn't birth those visions in an environment of old, stinking thinking. Over time, I changed my focus from the old mindset of things not working out to the new mindset of possibility and everything working in my favor. Now whenever I embark on a new endeavor, it's easier for me to spot when an old way of thinking is attempting to surface. I know that a new environment or new wine is forming and for the new skin to hold the new wine, I must release the old way of thinking and being. Old skins cannot hold new wine. Outdated beliefs and thought patterns are no place for expansion and infinite possibilities to take hold.

FEAR OF THE UNKNOWN

THERE IS A STORY I'D LIKE TO SHARE THAT SPEAKS TO fearing the unknown: A man was walking down the street and encountered a few people sitting on a porch. A dog laid on the porch, whining and groaning. The man asked what was wrong with the dog. One person replied, "Because he's lying on a nail." The man went on to ask, "Why doesn't he get up?" The person responded, "Because it's not hurting bad enough." The dog was used to being in an uncomfortable situation even though it caused him pain. The longer he stayed on it, the longer he experienced the pain and had become accustomed to the pain. The dog could've removed itself from the nail to be in a more comfortable position, yet it didn't because its pain had become familiar to him. Removing itself from the pain was a territory it wasn't used to, so instead it chose to remain with the familiar pain.

There are so many points that can be made with this story; however, the points I'll speak to are remaining in an uncomfortable situation and being unwilling to move "because it's not hurting bad enough." I can remember how I stayed in situations that I knew wasn't for me even it hurt my body, mind, and spirit. I didn't move on because I didn't know what would happen to me and I didn't trust the wonder and awe that would have come out of me moving on. In retrospect, I would have further along in life if I just trusted the Source within enough to move on. I would have been closer to my dreams, desires, and ideas a lot sooner.

I didn't let go of what ailed me because it was inconvenient to do so. Additionally, I believed that I wouldn't be able to stand on my own if I did. I feared what others would say about me if I stayed or if I left a situation. There was a relationship or routine that I developed with other people that we were familiar with. Because of that, I didn't want to rock the boat and I didn't want to draw attention to myself for making a change or a move to better my circumstances. I knew that there was something better for me, yet I didn't want to risk it being scrutinized by others. To move through this unknown, I began to repeat to myself, "It doesn't matter what people will say or think of me!" It seems simple, yet at times it's very difficult to agree to. For the co-creation process to take place, I had to make a shift in my mind to one where the only thing that mattered was what True Essence said. My focus shifted from the fear of the unknown, to God being all there is and nothing else.

WHAT IS THAT ONE THING?

Have you ever struggled with knowing which dream to focus on? I have. There have been so many ideas, visions, and dreams that were given to me, and I wasn't sure where to start and when. Then I realized that all I had to do was just start, and from there, I'd receive the guidance and experience that could be applied to the other dreams and visions I had. I chose my one thing, which was music, and from there, everything fell into place in its own timing. Once I was open to receive directions to fulfill one idea, vision or dream, other dreams, ideas, and visions began to appear.

That one thing took me to new levels I never anticipated. That one thing has rolled into endless possibilities for me to create music, write songs, and write books and to speak to millions of people about The Essential Peace of Life. I am like a growing tree with many branches and delectable fruit. I have created a new program for youth and a plethora of book ideas to write. I've also developed other programs and new platforms to convey my message. The one thing that I went for has opened doors for continuous creation and has led to the opportunity to help people realize their greatness that is already within them.

THE SUBCONSCIOUS AND CO-CREATING

I would like to share a mantra with you to help with the co-creating process: "I Am in alignment to receive more than I could ever ask or think." Now, how did that feel? I bet it felt great. Here is why I wanted you to say that: The subconscious mind gives directions to the conscious mind, and in the process of co-creating, those directions are what unfolds your dreams, ideas, and visions. The how may not look like the way that will bring you towards your intended end, yet it will. When there is a request for patience, would you receive patience or the opportunity to be patient? If there is a request for courage, would you receive courage or the opportunity to be courageous? Just because what you ask for doesn't come in the way it is expected, doesn't mean it isn't happening. Please don't turn away from you're asking for just because it's doesn't look the way you think it should. Everything is always working together for your good. What is that one thing, that one idea, one vision, one dream that you have? Plant it in your mind, and allow it to grow, branch off, and expand past your wildest imagination.

Another point about the subconscious mind when it comes to co-creating is that there is no concept of time. The passage of time, as we count it in minutes / hours / weeks / years is a human construct that helps us to keep track of our day-to-day existence. I'd often hear people say they are too old to follow their dreams. My thought on this is if we never had age to determine time on Earth, then we would never know by when something should occur. We wouldn't have this basis for measuring when things should be done and would be free to create at any time. I implore you to not worry about time and age. The infinite Universe knows your desires will happen at the appointed time. If you stay ready and focused, the process will happen. Even though it might be months from now, according to how we measure time, it's always the right moment according to the Universe. Everything occurs at the appropriate moment for the appropriate outcome. Everything works out just as it should when it should.

WRAPPING UP

THE UNIVERSE IS ALWAYS DOING WONDROUS THINGS and you are a part of it. And it is time for you to tap in. Listen to the ideas that are prepared especially for you. Don't allow the fear of the unknown, old beliefs that you may have created, and what people think of you to affect what's supposed to manifest in your life. I let the pain of my past keep me in a place where I didn't believe that I could do anything productive with my life. I spent a lot of time creating and doubting my abilities at the same time and really not getting anywhere at all. Now, that I know that my pain is here for me to learn and grow from, I have allowed myself to be open to what is right fully mine, I deserve it, and I'll allow it. Begin to open and allow all that is within you to come out. We only have this precious moment; let's get started and get it done. Everything we need, we have *right* now. The Universe only works in the *right now*. You're backed up by the Universe and you have everything that you need now at this very moment. Enjoy being a co-creator. It's your destiny and it will be great. Trust me, I'm a living witness.

7

YOUR WORD IS YOUR BOND

When I was involved in the multi-level marketing company, I had a hard time keeping my word. I had set some hefty visions and goals for myself, yet I didn't complete those goals. I asked my team to hold me accountable to hitting my goals, yet that didn't help. For two months straight, I worked sparingly and produced sparingly. I would get mad because I had put time into making appointments only for those people to cancel on me. I made follow-up calls to people who told me they would come to the weekly meetings only to not show up. And on the occasion, they did show up, they would be late and had no interest in joining the team. I expected a huge outcome from doing the bare minimum. I gave my word that I was going to complete a goal yet didn't put the correct effort into making it happen. I wasn't holding true to my word, and I didn't get the projected outcome that I had asked other people to hold me accountable for. I couldn't blame the people I met with, nor could I get mad at the people that didn't show up. I could only blame myself for my actions.

I had to realize that even though I had others holding me accountable, I really had to hold myself accountable. I was the only one responsible for the words that I put out into the atmosphere. I was the one who said what I wanted, and I was the one who didn't take the aligned actions to manifest what I wanted. In the end, I was the one hurt by not honoring my word to myself. And it sent a message that I wasn't a person of integrity.

WHY BONDING IS IMPORTANT

WORDS HAVE MEANING AND THEY HOLD WEIGHT. AND we are bonded to the words we speak. Let's look at the word bond. Bond means, "something that binds, fastens, confines, or holds together." When I speak, I have bonded myself with the Universe to co-create what I said I was going to do. I have made myself accountable for the words spoken. I must move on what I say and as I do, I experience the manifestation of my actions. This is not to bring pressure in my life; it's about creating the life that I have always wanted.

I have, through my word, agreed to be a part of a life-transforming process that will bless me and countless others. I said that I wanted to take this message of The Essential Peace of Life out into the world. By putting those words out into the Universe, I made an agreement that is now bonded. No matter how long it takes, this bond will remain in place until I've seen to the completion of it.

In previous chapters, I mentioned that I wanted to learn to create my own music and produce it. Because of that desire, I went to college and got a degree. Shortly after, I made the transition from Buffalo, New York, to Phoenix, Arizona, and it ended up being the change I needed for my life. I was presented with an opportunity to further enhance my skills of music creation, playing the piano, and singing. There was a music school around the corner from where my family lived and I started taking classes, which only took my skills to another level. I started performing in front of audiences and touching lives through my music.

After a few years in Arizona, I made the choice to

move to Los Angeles. Shortly after, I attended and joined Agape International Spiritual Center to become a Spiritual Licensed Practitioner. I have had this idea of being a beneficial presence on the planet through being an inspirational speaker and as an Agape Licensed Practitioner, I acquired a wealth of information and new ways to fulfill on that promise and desire. I held on to the ideas, dreams, and visions that I had, and they have expressed in ways I never expected.

What if I stayed in Buffalo and waited for someone to finally decide I was worthy to be taught what I needed to fulfill what I know that Essence has given me to co-create. I really didn't know what was to come for me and how my life would have unfolded, all because I was in place in my mind didn't allow me to be open to what my life could be, because I was stuck in my pain and wanting someone else to sooth it instead of myself.

What bonds have you created for yourself that you may have forgotten about? What words did you speak that you want to take form today? I encourage you to take the steps to remember and if you can't remember, create new bonds and stick with them. Trust me, the old bonds will resurface. I can still have the same goals I had for the network marketing business I was a part and use them in a different for form of expression and that's ok. The goal is to maintain the bonds that were and are created. Allow them to be the foundations to something great happening and unfolding in your life. The time is now to acknowledge them and co-create something wonderful.

YOUR WORDS HAVE POWER

IN CHAPTERS 5 AND 6 I MENTIONED HOW POWERFUL words are. Sticks and stones can break your bones, yet the words you speak if focused on long enough can have a real lasting effect on you. I have realized that when I speak, the Universe is creating what I am saying whether I want it to or not. It is the law of attraction at work. Words are key to the bonding process; they are the glue that holds what you say and what is manifested and how they are used matters. As previously mentioned, words are part of the activity of the conscious mind, and they put into action any and everything that is to be manifested. It's important to be clear when using words because they have meaning and can define who a person, place, or thing is and can be.

I know that being in pain while using my words

produced a lot of unproductive moments in my life. I had moments that I realized that I wasn't using my words to create my highest and best moments, yet I did know that I was trying to convey the pain that I was feeling, and I needed help to work through it. I had words of fury and they turned into anger fits and rage. I have seen firsthand how powerful words can be when I didn't have the proper language to express what I was feeling in those moments. It didn't help that I was being ignored, yet if I knew how to stand for myself and properly express what I was feeling and needed, I could have had a better outcome oppose to rage and anger fits, or not. I'm so grateful for grace and people coming to my add to show me how I can be great for me first and speak into my life what I want and make it so.

I have always been fascinated by words because of the vast amount to choose from and their different meanings and pronunciations. It also astounds me that there are words that share the same meaning as other words. It's amazing how language and words affect how anything, and everything happens.

Words help us get through the tough times. They inspire us when we need encouragement. Words help us to understand things that we didn't initially know. Most importantly, words help us communicate. Without words, our favorite songs wouldn't be created. Love poems wouldn't touch the hearts of loved ones. A joke wouldn't make us laugh or a sad story wouldn't make us cry. Besides being one with the Universe, nothing else holds more weight than the words that are used to communicate with Spirit via affirmations, meditation, visioning, and prayer.

I noticed the true power of words when I read Malcolm X's autobiography. While he was in prison, he read and learned every word in the dictionary and their meanings. He had a wonderful command of language and a broad vocabulary, and this came across in his speeches. This, to me, is the main reason he was so captivating as a person and speaker. I'm not at that point of reading the whole dictionary, yet any word that I come across and I don't know it, I will look it up. I realized that the words I speak have power and meaning and if not used properly, could be detrimental to my life. I like the song by Donald Lawrence titled, "I Speak Life." What I love most is that the song reminds us to not only speak life into someone else's life, yet also into our own lives. I've said it before, and I'll say it again for emphasis: Life and death are in the power of the tongue. As such, we should speak our words carefully.

INTEGRITY THROUGH TRUSTED COMMUNICATION

It's easy to forget and take for granted how much our words influence other people. What people say sticks with us, whether we want it to or not, and regardless of who speaks the words. There is a level of trust that is placed in the spoken word. Trust is huge and once it's broken, it's difficult to get it back.

When I was in the lower level of the church and I herd my mother state to her friend that I was a bad boy, that really stuck with me for a very long time in my life. I believe that I felt that what was really happening to me didn't matter, what mattered was how my mother saw me. It was very difficult to shake that off at the time because I never wanted my mother to be upset with me. Yet I did know that what was communicated at the moment wasn't true, because I was living my best life as a child and having the time of my life. I made a different choice and wanted my moms favor over my own sanity.

Integrity plays a huge part in communication. The word integrity means, "adherence to moral and ethical principles; honesty." Let's focus on the honesty part of the definition. I have discovered that when I speak, people believe what I say. They trust that what I say will direct them to the right path and that my words will help them in their manifestations. There is a sense of honesty that has been created between me and the listener.

Let's revisit an example from earlier that dealt with me giving my word to my multi-level marketing team to hit certain numbers. As we know, I didn't hold up my end of the bargain. I wasn't honest with myself first and I wasn't honest with the person I stated my vision to. My inability or lack of desire to honor what I said created distrust between me and the person holding me accountable. I knew things were bad when my accountability partner said, "I'll believe it when I see it." That wasn't a productive reaction to get, and I knew then that I had to either put up or shut up. If I say I'm going to do something and I don't put it to action, I create a form of dishonor through my communication. It could lead to people no longer believing a thing that I say from that moment on. Thankfully, I learned the value of doing what I mean and meaning what I say. It is a lesson I had to learn even though I learned it the hard way.

SPEAK LIFE INTO YOUR LIFE

I HAVE TALKED WITH PEOPLE WHO STATED THEY NEEDED to make changes to their bodies (for the better) yet would continue to model the same behaviors that kept them from bettering themselves. We all have heard the quote, "The definition of insanity is doing the same thing over and over and expecting a different result." This was exactly what those people were doing. I know from experience that it's not OK to stay stuck in mess. I also know how easy it is to remain stuck in mess. Honoring your word doesn't have to be hard. If you want to stop smoking because you know the harmful effects, then stop smoking. If you want to work out more and eat healthier, then workout and eat healthy. If you want a healthy and productive relationship, then put yourself in a position to receive that. It really is that simple.

I realized that I did put myself in a position where I hadn't spoken life into life for a very long time. I allowed what happened to me to be my story and how I should be known for. It wasn't until I started this journey of writing this book that I discovered the connection between my illness and the pain I was carrying and what it was doing to my communication skills. As I stated before if was by grace that I'm able to see that and make the necessary transformations to exhibit the life that I truly wanted and become what I have created to be. I'm not held to what happened or what was said before and able to speak a life that is flourishing and wonderful above and beyond.

WRAPPING UP

I REACHED A POINT IN MY LIFE WHERE I HAD TO understand that honoring my word was important. As a result, my whole world has transformed for the better. I take every opportunity to have integrity in everything I do. I think before I speak because I know the powers my word holds. I also learned that I must be true to what I say about myself. If I don't love myself enough to hold true to my words, how could my words hold true to anyone else? I started to affirm that I am a phenomenal person and saying so inspired me to take the steps that unveiled my greatness and worth. I held and continue to hold myself accountable to those words. Remember: You are connected to the most powerful energy source there is. You can do anything you say you can do. I believe that for myself and I also believe that for you.

8
ENJOY BEING WHO YOU ARE

I, like most people, have felt like I didn't fit in. I wanted to fit in so badly that I was willing to do anything it took to do so. At one point in my life, I didn't believe that I had what it took to be what I wanted to be because I believed what other people said about me and valued their opinions about me. It always seemed to feel like it was them that had a connection and I was the one of the only odd people out. Because of that feeling I wasn't wonderful enough as I was and that made me unlovable and unlikeable and that made me feel alone and angry. I didn't realize that I was already great, had what it took to make it, and I was liked and loved by something greater and bigger than everyone. I thought there was a cookie cutter way of being and doing that I didn't fit into. At that time, I didn't realize that I was great just the way I was. I didn't know that all I had to do was believe in myself and know that I am someone of value and importance, a commodity.

Society places weight and value in external validation and sadly, many have tried to meet this expectation. It's impossible to be who you are if you're constantly attempting to fit into a cookie cutter standard of you. Your worth is not dependent upon or measured by someone else's standards. After years of struggling with approval and validation from others, I started to realize that I was one with the power within. I became comfortable with the truth that who I am now is already awesome, great, wondrous, and fantastic and with that power, I can do and be anything. I had to begin to ask myself, "Why are you looking and allowing someone to tell you something different from your true self?" When I began to search for that answer, I was told something that I never forgot: Only you can unfold into a better you! I say this mantra every time I look in the mirror as it helps me to take responsibility for my life and the power that I am. It serves as a daily reminder that keeps me true to my path of co-creation. Anytime I start to doubt, I return to this phrase, and it gets me right back to center.

CREATED IN THE IMAGE AND LIKENESS

My Uncle Joe Peeler, my mother's brother, was a pastor and he spoke a sermon that my father always reminds me about. It was taken from Genesis 3:8-11 and speaks to the moment when The Divine found Adam and Eve in the Garden of Eden. Adam and Eve hid in the bushes, were naked, and scared after eating fruit from the Tree of Knowledge of Good and Evil. My uncle said The Divine asked Adam and Eve one important question, "Who told you that you where naked?" In other words, and to personalize this a bit, who told you that you aren't who you were created to be? If God, the wonderful and all powerful, didn't tell Adam and Eve (or you in this case) that something was incorrect about them, then who did? What made someone else's truth more important than the Divine One?

Let's think about this for a moment. You are created in the likeness and image of the One true creator of all. As that image, you are wonderfully created inside and out, with every exciting thing within you to do wondrous and exciting things. You have been stamped with the seal of approval by your Creator to be the best that you can be. As the likeness of God, you are already loved and appreciated for being who you are. There is no mistake in how you were created; you have a purpose. There is no one like you. The I am that you are is beyond anything that you could ever think or imagine.

I remember once when I worked as an assistant store manager at my first job. I was outgoing and personable, and our customers loved to come to the store when they saw that I was working the cash register. I didn't meet a person who I didn't introduce myself to and if we weren't friends, we at least knew each other when we saw each other. I was transferred to another store and assumed that I'd have the same interactions with the customers there. The customers there were not intrigued by my friendly and charming ways. I even felt that people looked at me cross-eyed and I didn't understand why. The new store manager at the location said that because I was a tall, African American man, and husky that I intimidated people. (Even though he knew I was as kind as a stuffed animal.) He believed my exterior was a threat and that my voice scared people off, too. This was news to me. To not cause further intimidation, I decided to be lowkey. This only worsened things because then customers started to complain that I was standoffish and disengaging. I realized that this was more about the new store manager than it was about me, so I returned to being my friendly self. I did my job the way I knew how and stayed true to myself. From that point own, I realized that I didn't have to change who I was to please anyone because who I was created to be was wonderful enough. More than that, what the manager said about me wasn't true and no longer mattered. I was able to come from behind the bush and accept the fact that God the Great One didn't tell me that me being African American, tall, husky and having a deep, sexy voice was intimidating. As a matter of fact, I was wonderfully created in the likeness and image of the Divine. And that is awesome enough for me.

GET ON THE FREQUENCY OF TRUTH

I'D LIKE YOU TO CONSIDER THESE QUESTIONS BEFORE WE continue: *Who told you that you weren't more than enough? Who told you that you don't have what it takes to be a better person? Who told you that you couldn't experience the fulfillment of the dreams, visons, and ideas that were given to you since the beginning of your life?* I had to ask myself these same questions. I had to answer them to get myself out the rut I placed myself in by valuing what others believed about me. It's not up to anyone else to tell me who I am, and I had to gain this understanding for myself. I understood that if something didn't feel pleasing when someone spoke to me, then it wasn't for my proper unfoldment. If what was said didn't vibe on the same frequency as the Divine, I knew that I couldn't allow it to rent space in my mind. I understood that if I focused on what was told to me and it didn't vibe with me, it had the potential of coming into fruition and potentially bringing me harm.

It's important to be on the same frequency as the True Essence within. When I'm continuously in tune with the Source within, I'm on the same wavelength as my Creator and reoccurring awesomeness comes with it. My frequency emits that awesomeness. The greatness, dreams, visions, and ideas all come from being on the same frequency of True Essence. So, it's imperative for me to stay in continual contact with True Essence.

As I began to understand what my dreams, visions, and ideas were, I realized I couldn't allow someone else's belief to alter or change the frequency of the truth that I am. Remember, we are created in the likeness and image of God and with that comes the validation of who we are and what we are meant to create in this life. Our daily challenge is to remain on the frequency of our Source. Our challenge is to remember that we have been created for greatness. Our challenge is to surrender to the truth that we are wonderfully and fearfully made for greatness.

I remember starting a new middle school in eighth grade. I was on the bus, heading back home, when a girl I didn't know and didn't know me said that no one liked me and that I didn't matter. For context, I was new to the school, and I suspect this made me an easy target to pick on. I didn't understand why she thought this, especially since I met some people earlier who were nice and seemed like they wanted to get to know me. Admittedly, her words did sting a little and I felt insecure. When I got home and told my mother how my day went, I shared with her what the girl said to me. My mother looked me right in the eyes and said, "I not only like you, I also love you. You do matter and that's all that matters." My mom was right, and the energy around what happened with the girl changed. I no longer gave attention to what the girl said and instead focused on what my mother said, which reflected the truth of who I was. Being in a new middle school was indeed a different world, and as a teenager, it was normal to look for confirmation from peers. I realized that this girl wasn't and wouldn't be a part of my inner circle of friends at school – what she thought and said didn't matter. I didn't have to see her again or be around her if I didn't want to. If I didn't take the time to remember the young man who I met on that first day named Shawn Dukes, who is one of my best friends, and my family, I would've stayed trapped in the falsity that I didn't matter. I do matter and people do like me. More importantly, just as much as people love me, I love myself even more and that is the greatest gift of all.

The Divine created each of us for greatness so there is no way that we should expect anything other than greatness. Adam and Eve didn't truly realize that they were only created for greatness and that everything about them was already perfect. They allowed someone to convince them of something that wasn't true about them. I believe the Great One already knew this would happen. That's why the Divine's glory was shown, and He didn't get rid of them and decide to start over with two new people to see if the outcome would be different.

The glory of the Great One is always revealing Itself to us – as us and through us. Albert Einstein, the greatest scientist of the 20th Century, recognized this when he said, "I want to know God's thoughts, the rest are just details." I remember when I had absolutely no choice but to hear the thoughts of the Divine because I was given up on as child by my parents. I had to learn the voice of the Divine and when I was being lead to do and be very productive and it sounded a lot like me. Yet, there were moments when I heard my voice and it wanted me to be unproductive which would be the voice of my ego wanting me to get my way no matter what. Once I learned the difference between the two, I was able to make choices that showed productivity. I am still having more work to do, yet my ratio is better than before. Whenever I knew for sure that I was guided and directed by the Divine, it was always done. Then I was able to trust the thoughts I am having about myself are of a splendid report.

I had this epiphany while writing this chapter that I want to share here: I realized that I am all that True Essence is. That is my true and ultimate identity. No one or nothing can make me think any differently. The Great One never told me any different, so that's what I believe. What someone thinks about me is none of my business. The Great I AM has the ultimate power to open and close doors. I know what's best for me because of my connection to the source within. And that's the only frequency that I'm aligned to.

THE PAST DOESN'T EQUAL YOUR FUTURE

Many people carry the pain and hurts of their past. I know because I was once one of those people. We carry the weight of what was said and done. We carry the weight of what we did to someone else. We carry the weight of the pain caused from hurting ourselves. We carry the weight of so many things that we cannot go back in time to change. There were thoughts that I allowed to take root in my mind that weren't productive for me. I allowed the things that were said to me about me to fester and replay in my mind. I allowed that to have power over what was true about me, which is what the Universe knows about me. Thankfully, before I got too lost in those thoughts, I heard a voice from within ask, "Who told you that you weren't great? Who told you that without them you couldn't amount to anything? Who told you that you weren't worth a plugged nickel? Who told you that you couldn't do what your heart and mind said you could? Who told you that you couldn't succeed? Who told you that you couldn't be the best you that you could be? I didn't tell you that. I will only tell you great and uplifting things. Since I haven't told you anything different, then there is nothing else to believe than the magnificent things that I have told you from the beginning of your life." If you heard this and it brings peace to your soul, which report you would believe? The one of Source or the one from someone who doesn't even know you? I'm sure you already know which one I chose to listen to.

Let's revisit an example I've shared in earlier chapters when I would have epileptic seizures. If you recall, when the seizures took place, the adults and people around me would say that I was doing it for attention and that I was a "bad child." It wasn't just the words that impacted me; it was also the actions with the words that made it difficult to receive the help I needed. What I believed about myself from then on had an impact on my life and could've been detrimental to my life. What direction could I have gone in? What effect would I have had in other people's lives: Would I be a blessing or a terror? I had a few choices. First, I could have been a disorderly child and been a disappointment to my family. Based on what I was told, I could have become a gang banger or drug dealer. I could have flunked out of school. Those actions could have led me to being homeless, in jail, or probably dead. Second, I could have fallen in a deep abyss of depression and took my own life. This option did cross my mind. I remember having an argument with my parents and instead of them being open to hear what I had to say, they ignored me. When I pulled a knife out of the drawer and stated that I would cut myself, they didn't even budge. I continued to believe that my life didn't matter and that I wouldn't succeed. Third, I could listen to the Source within and prove those untruths wrong. I could show myself first that I am a wonderful child. I would have to find ways to keep myself active and become very productive in creative ways like writing, painting, singing, playing an instrument, and sports. I would have to do some extra studying or get a tutor if needed, to get my grades up. In essence, I had to be my No. 1 fan.

I'm sure you guessed that I chose the third choice and found a way to become the best child that I could be for me. I discovered what needed to be changed for me to accomplish great things in my life. I learned to be a great listener and observed from other relationships how to relate. I remembered what seemed negative in those relationships and practiced the positives that seemed to work. Joy became a priority in my life. I did what I could to make the best for my life, with or without the support of family. I followed the way of True Essence. I may not have done everything correctly on my journey, yet I made it a practice to do whatever it took to gain understanding of what was rightfully mine and I went for it.

Returning to the story of Adam and Eve, I realize

that they never truly understood who they were or that everything the Divine had was already theirs. Everything was already theirs and they didn't have to want for anything at all because of who they were. They didn't know, yet I am grateful that we get to know this truth. You don't have to want for anything and all that the Father has is yours. So, I ask you again: Who told you that you couldn't have what rightfully belongs to you? It's all simple: If the Great One didn't tell you, then it's not true. If the frequency feels off and it goes against a great feeling you have, then it's not true. There is more in you than you know, and you must learn to see it for yourself.

AFFIRM + ATTRACT YOUR TRUTH DAILY

I HAVE MENTIONED THE IMPORTANCE OF AFFIRMATIONS throughout this book. I believe in affirmations so much that I created an online show, "Let's A.M.P. Up," which includes affirmation, meditation, and prayer. I host this on Instagram and Facebook live every Monday and Friday morning. Through A.M.P., the viewers are supported in communing with their inner power and encouraged to be in continuous communication with Spirit. When I taught preschool,

I had my afterschool students do daily affirmations before we got started with homework. They would say, "I love myself. I am an important person. Great things are supposed to happen in my life." I loved watching their faces light up every time they affirmed these truths about themselves. Now you can adopt this same affirmation, or you can say the following, "I AM wonderful!" This one-line affirmation captures the entire truth about you! Affirmations bring clarity, peace, and calm to the mind and soul. Affirmations also open you to the greatness that is available and connects you to the Source within. You are wonderful, you are important, and great things are meant to happen in your life. Please know this.

When I say, "I AM," not only am I speaking about myself, I'm also speaking of the True Essence within. I AM acknowledges my connection to the Source within and constantly affirms the truth of my nature. When you speak about the grandness of yourself, you're also speaking about the grandness of True Essence. Our words manifest into our lives exactly what we think and speak. So, when you say, "I AM" be sure that it is followed with positive, uplifting, and encouraging words as everything that follows I AM affirms the truth of who you are.

This also falls within the lines of the "Law of Attraction." This principle has been discussed in a book and video called, "The Secret" and by Jerry and Ester Hicks who have produced multiple books, CDs, and videos on the subject. The Law of Attraction teaches that what a person thinks and says influences what they experience. This law establishes that you draw to you your dominant thought, belief, and feelings. Whatever is truly wanted and desired – sweet or unsavory – will come into fruition. The Law of Attraction opened my eyes to the unlimited possibilities my life had to offer. I learned a new way of thinking and learned more about my true power.

BREAK FREE FROM THE MENTAL BONDAGE

I KNOW FIRSTHAND HOW EASY IT IS TO LET NEGATIVE motives become the focus of my life, especially in the work environment. At one point, I allowed someone's negative thoughts, comments, and behavior influence my life. I worked for a pre-K educational program as a teacher's assistant. I wanted to move up in the organization and work in the office to put my true skills to use. I thought that everything was going to be better in this new position. I knew I had people skills and the ability to relate when needed. I thought that having a sales background and customer service abilities were great strengths to have. I ended up getting the position, which meant an increase in salary, my own office, and more peace at work (or so I thought). This upgrade wasn't welcomed by all. Someone whom I thought was a positive acquaintance came to me within the first week of the new position and said that I wasn't fit for the position and was better off working with children. I later discovered this person spread rumors about me to other employees.

Since this person was part of the administration team, tasks were sometimes given to me without my understanding on how to complete them properly. When I would ask for help, there was only one person I could go to and even that person wasn't any help. To top it off, I was frustrated because I wasn't properly trained for the position. Unfortunately, I allowed what happed at the office to affect my company and home life. I broke down and wanted to get away from everything. I allowed what someone else thought of me to affect me deeply (a life lesson) and I didn't feel at ease. I had to shift my thinking quickly and did so by remembering why I took the position to begin with. And then I received some insight from my mentor, Chris Roland, that helped pull me out of the mental dungeon I was in. "You're not keeping your attention on what you truly want for your life." He was right. I turned away from what True Essence said about me and placed my worth in other people's opinions. I was already productive enough to do whatever I put my hands on. Once that was reaffirmed, I became calm and reassured.

In the end, I was removed from the position. It's OK to remove yourself from what isn't serving you. This experience taught me that it's better to put my feelings and respect first. It also taught me to be mindful of how I allow things that happen to spill over into other areas of my life. What was meant to harm me became the very thing that helped me grow more as a person, a leader, and friend.

WRAPPING UP

Who told you that you couldn't do what the Great One already has said that you could? Who told you that you weren't perfect just the way you are? When Adam and Eve took their attention off the grandness of Source and focused on something other than that grandness, they lost the understanding of their true selves and the great destiny that was theirs. They listened to someone other than their creator and believed that the Divine would be ashamed of them.

They didn't realize that they were already living in the fullness of God and that all God saw was the glory that they were. When you begin to understand the truth about yourself, you will do better for yourself and others. It's wonderful if you have to continue to remind yourself of this, because this is a practice and it comes with being comfortable with who and who's you are. Learn to be comfortable with the voice that sounds like you, guiding, directing, and reminding you who you truly are. As you embrace the truth of who you are, then nothing outside of what your Creator has said about you can shape, mold, or sway you from what the Universal One knows and has determined is true about you.

9
YOU ARE A LEADER TOO

Being a leader is something that I have always wanted to understand, learn, and be. Leadership is a subject that's special to me. I grew up around men and women who I saw as leaders yet when I approached them for advice, they didn't teach me. They came from a time where you had to work yourself up the ladder before you could consider yourself a leader. They believed that you had to be a follower first before stepping into leadership. Some of them even believed that to be considered a leader, you had to be chosen. Even though I knew that I was a true leader, I often wandered how long I would have to follow. I wondered when I would get my chance to lead.

I had to get clear on what I wanted to accomplish as a leader. I also had to understand why I was fighting to be a leader. Then it hit me: I didn't have to fight anyone to be a leader. My predecessor's journey and leadership approach weren't mine and I had to find my own. I had to create my own journey and following. In doing so, I had to understand what I wanted and how I could bring forth what was already inside me. How could I become the leader that I was destined to be? I had to understand my role as a leader and what that meant – for me.

THE MEANING OF BEING A LEADER

As I listened to my associate's concerns and the Spirit within, I began to have a vision of what would become The Essential Peace of Life. Even when I thought I was done getting the download the first time, I would receive additional information to add every now and again. It never seemed to end. When I looked over what I had written, I felt a deep sense of purpose. My vision expanded and I saw myself presenting to a large crowd and they were receptive to the information I was presenting. I knew then that The Essential Peace of Life was preparing me to be the leader I was meant to be. A leader that will help people heal from their past pains and open their minds to a greater awareness of a more productive and prosperous life. The more this vision revealed what was to come, the more I desired to understand leadership.

As I researched leadership, a few questions naturally surfaced for me to ponder. *What does it mean to be a leader? What qualifies me to be a leader? Do I already have what it takes? Do I need to be in a certain field, job position, or be appointed with the right characteristics to be a leader?* This desire to prepare for leadership led me to the answers and I discovered that what I was searching for had been within me all along. I just had to develop it.

According to the dictionary, a leader is, "a person or thing that leads; a directing, guiding head; a person of influence." To lead means, "to go before or with to show the way; conduct or escort; to conduct by holding and guiding; to influence or induce and to guide in direction, course, action, opinion." From these definitions, I concluded that everyone can be a leader. These definitions didn't state that there were specific qualifications needed to lead or that I needed to be appointed by someone. It did state that there had to be a destination, idea, or vision that people are being led to. I knew in my heart of hearts that I wanted to lead, yet I didn't know how and where to lead people. The Essential Peace of Life came into my life once I started to ask how I could lead and what was mine to give. As I asked the questions, the answer came and served as a framework for how and where I would lead people.

In *The Spirit of Leadership* by Dr. Myles Munroe, he states, "Leaders inspire by expressing their inner passion, which then resonates with others and causes them to join in pursuing the leaders' visions." I had the biggest aha moment after reading that. I created The Essential Peace of Life to help heal people and to serve as a guide that helps them unfold consciously and that is what being a leader is all about. It's about "being a beneficial presence on the planet," as Rev. Michael Beckwith would say. After reading that excerpt, I realized that I was a person of influence. I had the life experiences that I learned from and could develop it in a way that would help others to transform their lives. I was relieved to discover that I didn't have to be chosen by someone else to be a leader. The obstacle that would hold me back from being a leader would be myself if I allowed it. I had what it took to help others through The Essential Peace of Life. With this awareness, I began to live my life as a leader.

ENVISION YOUR IDEA

While doing the research on leadership, I understood that I had to have an idea or platform. It wasn't enough for me to want to be a leader; I had to have an end in mind. I needed to know where I was going and how to take people with me. I needed an idea. So, what is an idea? An idea is, "any conception existing in the mind as a result of mental understanding, awareness, or activity. A thought, conception, or notion. An impression." The idea that is given comes from True Essence. When something comes to mind, its presence lets you know that it can be accomplished by and through you. I believe every Idea is unique to the individual who received it and is theirs to create and share. This is one of the reasons why I feel leadership is everyone's birthright: Those who want to take advantage of doing wondrous things will do what it takes to bring their idea into fruition.

I suspect that most people have something they want to do with their lives and have an idea of what it looks like. They may not, however, be clear on how to get started. They can see the idea yet might be uncertain on how to allow it to unfold. Habakkuk 2:2 in the Bible offers some insight. "... Write the vision and make it plain upon tablets so he may run who reads it." This scripture advises to write down the idea and take the steps to make the message plain for others to understand and run forward with. In this case write the Idea and do what it takes to make it plain so that the message of what's to can be carried forth. Meditation and journaling also help to make the vision plain. Taking time to be one and commune with Source is invaluable and can yield strategies, thoughts, and visions that will support you in making the vision plain. In the silence, in that sweet communion with Source is where communication takes place. In the silence is where Ideas and visions from True Essence are revealed. When I spend time in the silence, I experience joy because I know that what I'm seeing is my true destiny to fulfill. And my journal is right next to me so that I can capture all the wisdom flowing through.

While being on the multi-level marketing team, I realized that having my own ideas was the key to being a leader. Even though I would bring people on to the team, they still looked to me to lead them in the right direction with a clear vision. I know for a fact that people are drawn to someone with a vision, someone who will impart change in great ways in their lives and the lives of countless others. I learned a valuable lesson while on that team: My ideas are only as effective as my belief in it. You must be convinced of it first before anyone else will want to be part of it. The idea is something that I had to believe in so much that no one can tell me that it isn't going to work. I had to love this idea so much that others would begin to love it, too. I also realized the value in bringing my whole unique self to the team as this is what inspired people to join. You are the secret ingredient – the hot pepper that makes your idea a winning recipe. Bring all of you to the vision and it will come to pass.

When I opened to the idea that was presented to me, I sat in the silence and learned what I needed to know to move forward. Although I wasn't fully into meditation at the time that The Essential Peace of Life came through, I had an enjoyable understanding of how Spirit communicated to me. I knew when I got this idea to create this program and the book, that I was given something groundbreaking to create. Are you familiar with how Spirit communicates with you? I've come to learn that the voice of Spirit is calm and like the voice of a mother – you know it when you hear it. This practice of listening is very essential as it serves as the channel through which you receive ideas and the wisdom on how to manifest it.

DEVELOPING THE IDEA

ONCE THE IDEA WAS RECEIVED, I HAD TO FORMULATE and develop it so that it made sense. When developing an idea – and before presenting it – you must be able to show its capabilities, possibilities, and its effectiveness. I'm reminded of when I was at Villa Maria College and enrolled in a business class. I learned how to create a business and marketing plan to pitch to potential investors. Each plan detailed to investors how valuable and beneficial the business would be to them and others. I learned how to break the idea down in a way that made it understandable and relatable. The same goes for your vision. While I'm not saying that you should write a business or marketing plan, what I am saying is that it's important to understand your vision from all angles and be able to communicate that. I am emphasizing how important it is to write the vision and make it plain.

When I first created The Essential Peace of Life, it was an outline that covered areas I felt were integral to maintaining peace. Even though I had the idea and outline, it wasn't ready for human consumption. It took some time to flush out all various sections and as I did, I began to share what I had with others. The feedback I received was invaluable and provided me the direction on how to improve the program. Their feedback gave me the opportunity to ensure the message was clearly conveyed and didn't have any blocks that would prevent the listener from receiving it. It was one thing to have the download, yet it was equally imperative to have additional facts to help back it up. As I developed the outline, I was able to create branches of different talks all centered on the foundation of The Essential Peace of Life.

A leader knows the ins and outs of the idea that he/she wants to convey. He also knows the importance of being a student as well as a master. Both are needed to teach others and to help create leaders. There is always time and room to learn.

After the development phase, is the execution stage. The word **execute** means, "to carry out, accomplish, to perform or do, to produce in accordance with a plan or design." An idea is nothing if it isn't executed. The execution process takes time, energy, and revisions, and only strengthens the idea. That's why it is important to take the idea and develop it into a plan of action that people can see and experience. While developing The Essential Peace of Life, I presented it at youth events in Niagara Falls, New York, even though it was still in the development phase and gleaned so much wisdom to further shape and strengthen the program. To me, this is the fun part because I can really be myself. I have fun presenting to others and sharing in the joy of the information presented. It feels wonderful to see the impact that being obedient to an idea has, not just in my life, yet in the lives of others.

∽

DUST YOURSELF OFF AND TRY AGAIN

On October 19, 2009, in Buffalo, New York, I attended a training for a sales position at the Atrium building for HSBC. The trainer said something that stood out to me. She said, "No, it is not personal. It's just no!" She continued to tell a story about Colonel Sanders, the founder of Kentucky Fried Chicken, and how he endured thousands of rejections before he found a restaurant that gave him a chance to make and sample his chicken recipe. The trainer went on to ask, "How many of you had ideas and dreams that you presented to someone, and that person told you no?" I was one of 5 people who raised my hand. The trainer continued, "Now is the time to dust off those old ideas and bring them back out, tweak them, and run with them."

I was floored and if I was in the church of my youth, I would have been shouting all over the place. Who knew that at that moment, I would receive guidance from Source through the trainer to go back to the drawing board and revive the ideas I pushed away and neglected – all because someone else said no? God knew. And that's how Spirit works. It was time for me to revive those ideas so that others would be blessed by them. I believe that these ideas are ours to worship in spirit and in truth, because we are a part and one with True Essence. We experience the glory of God when we follow and are obedient to the vision that desires to birth through us. I encourage you to be open, ready, and willing to hold on to and execute your vision even when faced with countless closed doors and rejections. You are one with True Essence; it's already done, and everything is working together for your good.

WHAT MAKES A LEADER?

PEOPLE SHARE QUOTES, WORDS OF WISDOM, LEARNING experiences, and advice to other people every day. The sharing of knowledge, to me, also qualifies a person to be a leader. If the information shared helps to open another person's eyes and steers them onto a much greater path towards fulfillment, then the person who delivered the information is a leader.

Therefore, I'm convinced that leadership isn't something that can be bestowed upon by another person. If a person possesses knowledge and passed along the information and experiences to another, that qualifies him or her as a leader in my book.

When I was with the multi-level marketing company – that has been mentioned several times throughout this book – I had an increased desire to be considered a leader. I wanted my name to be mentioned and sealed among the elite. I worked hard, fought through every challenge that confronted me, and more just to be considered a leader. The harder I tried to be a leader, the harder I had to work for it. There were always more metrics that needed to be achieved before I was considered a leader by those in the company. I did everything I could to impress them. I even moved to another city in hopes of attaining the title in the next level. I had a fire in me, and I was determined to "earn" leadership. Sadly, I went nowhere fast in the company even with all the effort. As my work went unnoticed, I started to resent the company and became very upset. I didn't realize at that time that I had turned away from my true calling and was trying to find fulfillment in something that wasn't meant for me.

There was a gentleman I was bringing into the business who pulled me aside after a meeting. He said, "This isn't going to be the outlet where your greatness is going to be expressed." When he first said this to me, I disagreed. I was invested in the company and learned a lot by being in the company. I saw how beneficial being on the team was to my life. I felt that I had to stay to earn my way to the top and that I would do so through hard work. The gentleman ultimately was right. A few months later, I was kicked off the team twice (the first time because of a misunderstanding). The second time, I took the dismissal as a sign that it was time to pursue my true destiny.

It was in that moment that I realized that I was a leader. I had to realign with True Essence to receive all that was rightfully mine. For the longest time, I thought that if I continued to be part of the company that they would give me the leadership title that I longed for. I sought validation from someone else to get something that I already was. I didn't realize that I was already a leader, that I already had something to bring forth to the world. I didn't realize that I would be a blessing in my own way. I was already chosen to express the co-created ideas that were within.

The path of leadership isn't for a select few. Any and everyone can awaken to their leadership potential. I am reminded of a quote by the late Dr. Martin Luther King Jr. that says, "Life's most persistent and urgent question is, what are you doing for others?" As a leader it isn't about what someone can do for you, it's about what you can do for someone. No one cares how much you know, until they know how much you care. The ideas that you are co-creating with Source are ideas that will help people awaken to their greatness.

WHAT DOESN'T MAKE A LEADER?

I HAVE ASSISTED SEVERAL LEADERS IN MY LIFE AND consequently, I've seen what works and what doesn't in leadership. I've seen leaders talk to those they were leading in harsh tones. I've seen leaders act as if they had dominion over other people's lives. I've seen leaders try to diminish the very people they were leading. Even as a leader, the Golden Rule should be understood and practiced: Do unto others as you would have others do unto you.

I also saw that some leaders were just doing what was done to them. This is when it is important to discover the ways that make you effective and positive as a leader. We don't have dominion over other people; as leaders, we are here to aid and guide. It's not up to us to discourage and dilute the hopes and dreams of others. Motivational speaker and author Earl Nightingale stated, "If you believe you can enrich yourself by diluting others, you can only end by diluting yourself." People will not want to be part of a vision where they're being discouraged in the process. It just won't work. People will follow the leader who moves with integrity, the one who encourages them in bringing out their greatness. No one cares how much you know until they know how much you care. Once people see and know that the idea of the leader is worth following, it's up to the leader to make sure that the path is ready for the people and will be a blessing for them.

WRAPPING UP

You are a leader. Being a leader is part of your inheritance and it is given to you by Spirit and not anyone else. You do not need the validation or permission from anyone because it was already given to you by Spirit, the True Essence within. Your only job is to co-create, to bring forth those ideas and dreams that will ignite and inspire the dreams in others. Being a leader is your right. Don't deny who you are any longer. Be a leader.

10

IN MIDST OF THE HURT THINK POSITIVELY

∼

Everything that an individual wants to manifest depends on their thoughts. Earl Nightingale wrote the following in *The Strangest Secret*, "The mind is like soil. No matter what you put in it, it will put out in great abundance whatever you put in the soil." We can't control the thoughts that come in, yet we can control how and if we focus on those thoughts. Our thoughts are like seeds in the soil. The longer we water them, or pay attention to them, the more they grow – and this is true for positive and negative thoughts. I am still working to perfect the art of positive thinking. When I stay on track, the outcome is wonderful. If I don't stay on track, the outcome is messy, and it takes time and effort to clean up what I've created. I had so much pain that I was focusing on that I created thoughts that weren't productive for my life. I allow my pain to have a mind of its own and I created so much that wasn't serving my personal growth and unfoldment. I didn't have high thoughts for my life and what was possible for me to make it in life. Yet the longer stayed open and available to wanting to know what it takes to be who I am supposed to be, I would get tools and practices on what it would take to affectively plant the thoughts that would allow me to have a new and productive way of thinking and being. The beauty is in the daily practice and in reassuring yourself that life is bountiful, beautiful, and joyous and only wants to work out for your productivity.

WHAT IS A POSITIVE ATTITUDE?

So, what does positive mean? Positive means, "moving forward or in direction of increase or progress; displaying certainty; acceptance; or affirmation, confident in opinion or assertion." And then there's the word attitude. Attitude means, "manner, disposition, feeling, position, expressive of an action." When both words are used together, they reflect the nature and expression of the True Essence within. Positive attitude describes a person's demeanor and is supported by his actions. This includes their body language and facial expressions. A person who has a positive attitude reflects an irrefutable faith and truth that despite what the eyes see, and the ears hear, everything is as it should be and is working for your productivity.

I learned and continue to learn about the power of positive thinking in bringing forth The Essential Peace of Life. I had to train myself to see this program as already done. As I did, the wheels were set in motion for the idea to take form, which allowed me to meet people who would help me fulfill the vision. Something to note: Your mindset is the environment that either supports or negates the idea that you are creating. This is why a positive attitude is crucial because it sets a thriving environment for all you need to be drawn to you. The movie *The Secret* confirmed this. The vibrations of your thoughts create your outward experience. A positive attitude creates the environment for wonderful things to happen. Yes, there will be time when fear, doubt, and worry will creep in, and that is normal. The challenge is to reframe where you're placing your attention and focus on the greatness that is unfolding as you continue to say yes to the vision. Staying positive helps you to stay on track despite the temporary hiccups that come with manifesting your dreams.

∼

WHAT IS A THOUGHT?

THOUGHT, WHICH IS THE ACT OF THINKING, MEANS, "to have or formulate in the mind, intention, purpose, to believe, to expect, to call to mind, to visualize, and meditation." To me, thoughts are how we communicate with True Essence. When looking at the definition, it is amazing to see the power that a thought has. A thought has the power to create and co-create whatever is in mind. This powerful frequency is a foundation for mostly everything that takes place on Earth. And as humans, we can tune into the powerful frequency and create anything because of it.

I read in the book *Mental Equivalent* by Emmet Fox about the power of a thought, which he refers to as "mental equivalent." In it he says, "The key to life is to build the mental equivalents of what you want and to expunge the equivalents of what you do not want. You build the mental equivalents by thinking quietly, constantly, and persistently of the kind of thing you want." A person's world is their mental equivalent. They create their world based on the thoughts they focus on. Isn't it empowering to know that as soon as you have a particular thought, you can focus on one that fits what you want?

MONITOR YOUR THOUGHTS

THE PREEMINENT LEADER OF INDIAN NATIONALISM IN British-ruled India, Mahatma Gandhi stated, "Men often become what they believe themselves to be. If I believe I cannot do something, it makes me incapable of doing it. Yet when I believe I can, then I acquire the ability to do it even if I didn't have it in the beginning." We are the co-creators, the masters of our outcome. What we think affects our outcomes and those around us. This is very important.

I'm a Star Wars fan. No matter who Obi Wan Kenobi was training – whether Anakin or Luke Skywalker – he would tell them to be mindful of their thoughts. He emphasized to the trainee that if they weren't mindful of their thoughts, their thoughts could betray them. If not careful, our thoughts have the potential of taking us into places we'd rather not visit. Angry feelings mixed with negative thoughts can be detrimental, especially when expressed through action. The great thing is that you change your thoughts and feelings just as quickly as you received the initial thought and feeling that caused the discomfort. Staying focused on positivity helps shift your world for the better.

DAILY PRACTICES

THERE ARE A FEW PRACTICES I HAVE INCORPORATED into my spiritual journey that helps me maintain a positive attitude. The first one is to maintain a grateful attitude. "Of all the attitudes we can acquire," wrote the late motivational speaker Zig Ziglar, "surely the attitude of gratitude is the most important and by far the most life changing." Giving thanks is very crucial to maintaining positive thinking. Giving thanks through any situation keeps a person calm. With gratitude, the focus is taken off the negative and redirected to something more pleasant. Gratitude helps us remain in the present moment and grateful for the present moment. If you think about it, in this moment is all that anyone will ever need. Once you start to think about something that happened or something that is needed in the future, then you take yourself away from what is here now. I know for a fact that focusing on this moment is extremely powerful. Being in the moment allows me to open to the ideas that will take care of any present needs and will care for any concerns and needs to come. Jesus understood how powerful thoughts were. He broke the loaves of bread and poured wine for 5,000 people. All he did was give thanks for what he had, and the multitude were fed. There were people around him who had thoughts of lack, yet Jesus stayed true to himself and his understanding that only thoughts of abundance would solve the issue. You, too, have that ability. You must foster a practice of having a positive mindset. You can cultivate this by giving thanks for what you have in this present moment.

The second practice is to meditate. Meditate means, "to engage in thought or contemplation; reflect and to engage in transcendental meditation, spiritual introspection." Philippians 4:8 of the Amplified Version of the Bible gives you instructions on what to meditate on. It states, "Whatever is true, whatever is worthy or reverent and is honorable and seemly, whatever is just, whatever is pure, whatever is lovely and lovable, whatever is kind and winsome and gracious, if there is any virtue and excellence, if there is anything worthy of praise, think on and weigh and take account of these things (fix your minds on them)." This is the time when you are communicating with the True Essence within. To support your meditation, you can play soothing instrumental music to facilitate the process. You can meditate for 10-15 minutes or longer at any time of the day. The most important thing is to set aside time to commune with True Essence and to receive the wisdom that emerges during that time.

The last practice is to be mindful of the thoughts you entertain. Remember, thoughts are important, and they have power. Whatever you focus on becomes your reality. because what is thought of and focused on will become reality. How is this for something to focus on: You live a great, abundant, prosperous, generous, and productive life. Your life is for the creating. There is a mission that was predestined in you by Source. Felt exciting, didn't it? Say this to yourself daily and begin to affirm it during meditation and notice the difference in how you feel about your life.

Being mindful of your thoughts also affects how people treat you. With a simple switch in the thought process, you will begin to affirm what is true about yourself, and it will reflect in how people treat and respond to you. This also helps you to take your focus off negative thinking and thoughts. When learning to speak well of yourself, everything else responds to the new pattern. A resource I recommend is The Perfect Power by Jack Addington. This book contains 30 days' worth of prompts that will help you build a positive mindset. It's a great resource of affirmations that would complement your daily meditations.

WRAPPING UP

A POSITIVE ATTITUDE CAN CREATE GREAT MIRACLES IN your life. Like meditation and gratitude, positive thinking positions you for a positive and peaceful life. I encourage you to really dig into this process. It will move you forward into a joyful place, where peace is always possible. This process will allow you to become stronger in an area that has been neglected in the past to create your desired present. Do what it takes to get out of the rat race of confusion and come into a more positive state of Peace. You deserve it!

11

BE YOU BY BEING PEACE

∼

Everything mentioned in the previous chapters comes down to this one concept: Being peace. In the consciousness of peace, there is the ability to think, listen, and move with ease. It's in the consciousness of peace that I realized a lot of my manifestations and open doors were revealed. In the consciousness of peace is where I'm continuously in tune with the True Essence and can receive clear directions. Peace was indeed the one thing I wanted to cultivate in my life of Pain. I wanted more than anything to have peace when it came to my parents and how they saw me due to my illness. Peace when it came to what and how I believed other people saw me based on what was communicated to them by my parents. And Peace for me just to know and be me fully and completely. More than anything I just wanted to life my best life without any obstructions and the only way to do that was to release what I thought I knew to be true based on the pain of my past and see my life bigger, brighter, and bolder, in the current moment. I had to be the peace that I wanted to reveal in and as my life.

There are many definitions for the word peace yet I'm going to highlight the ones that represent what I'm conveying in this chapter. Peace means, "Freedom of the mind from annoyance, distraction, anxiety; a state of tranquility or serenity, silence, stillness." I live by and strive to live in peace daily. Peace is my awareness of my true self. When I'm peace, I find the answers to my pressing questions. Although I believe in receiving counsel from others, it's 10 times better to be tapped into and receive the wisdom from the one true Mind.

AWAKENING TO THE PEACE WITHIN

Since I have started focusing on peace as my nature and experience, I have started functioning on a higher level. I won't say that I have overcome every obstacle, yet I have gotten better at being more aware of pivoting when challenges do come. With this new sense of understanding, I'm also able to keep my anger in check. I'm more cognizant of how my reactions affect my day-to-day. From the moment I was perceived as a bad child by my mom, I have lived with an illusion of who I thought and knew myself to be. If there was a moment when I felt like I wasn't holding up to being a wonderful child, then I would default to thinking that I was a bad child. I didn't know how to handle or protect myself from situations properly at that time and anger became my first response. I turned to anger – emotionally and physically – because I thought that was how things were supposed to be handled.

I liken this to The Incredible Hulk. Even though he is a fictional character, his experience is somewhat similar to how I – and most people – respond when we don't have the proper coping skills. The Incredible Hulk is a man first and monster second. (His name is David Banner or Bruce Banner depending on when you were introduced to the character.) Banner was exposed to gamma radiation and thus The Incredible Hulk was created. Each time that he was negatively provoked, Banner would transform into a green beast. To some, he seemed harmful and mean, yet to those who knew him, he was still kind and wanted the best for people. While trying to search for treatments to kill the beast within, he found a way to keep himself at peace to contain it and ensure no harm or trouble was caused. He accomplished this by meditating and keeping his mind focused and clear. This also allowed him to be more aware and kept him from situations that would cause him to react in a negative way, thus releasing the beast.

I have learned to keep the beast in check to have a better direction and outcome for my life. I realized that I didn't accomplish much when I was angry. Although I can't kill the beast, I can be open to the information it is giving me. I found more productive ways to express without losing control and overreacting. I allowed my anger to be my ally.

In the moments when I wasn't exuding my peaceful nature, I noticed a few contributing factors. The first factor is that I placed my attention on the problem or the illusion of a problem. All I could see were the issues and not the answers. My thoughts were scattered, and I was moving further off the path of manifesting the greatness within me. The longer I kept my attention on the illusion of a problem, the longer it took me to realize that I didn't have to stay in that space. I recall an issue that surfaced in my life that seemed to happen unexpectedly. I needed some extreme guidance; all I knew to do was talk about it to whoever would listen, which gave the illusion more attention and made it even more real. I gave that illusion so much power that it made me sick, literally. I worried so much about the problem and gave it all my attention that I would get headaches. This frightened me; I couldn't believe how much I had changed from a fun, easygoing person, to a frustrated and angry person who nobody wanted to be around. My attitude and energy levels were low, and I didn't even want to listen to the Source within. I was disruptive to myself, and it ruined a lot of my relationships.

I realized that I wasn't going to get the answer from an outside source because I wouldn't have listened. I had to calm myself down and go within for the answer. I knew that I had to do this if I wanted the illusion of the problem to end. I had to remember that it's not by my might and not by my power; it's by the Spirit within. I took the time to relax and give thanks. In my meditation I would say, "You are the one and only true source of my life and I trust only you." I repeated this multiple times. I had to surrender to wanting to solve the problem. I had to turn my attention to productive positive thoughts and what brought joy to my life. I had to let go completely.

Rev. Michael Beckwith wrote in his book, *Life Visioning*, that, "surrendering is yielding to your excellence." He also stated that, "in the act of surrendering, you no longer allow patterns of negativity to take over. Begin yielding to peace and every productive thing that comes with it." After I read that, I let go of the belief that things were being done to me. I started to allow greatness to overtake me, which is my rightful inheritance. When I switched my attention off the illusion of the problem, I became more coherent to what was going on around me. With that, I moved closer to the manifestation of my dreams, visions, and ideas. This is also true when the focus is taken off the illusions of fear, doubt, worry, not being enough, not feeling loved, not having enough money, etc. Anything that isn't in alignment with you being and feeling that you are Peace. Know that there is always a reason for those feelings to show up and it's our job to know why so that we can stand tall and see the best of our lives through those illusions of problems.

A transformation happened because I decided to surrender. I then became aware of peace and my focus was on the Source of all good in my life. The light came on; the answer came to my attention. I was amazed how instantaneously wonderful my mood felt. The change in my attitude for life and my energy level all increased for the better. I wanted peace and productiveness to be my everyday way of life and I placed my attention on that. I began to receive the feeling of peace that discredited all the comfort I found in the illusion of the problem. I discovered the problem wasn't a real problem and didn't have any power. The problem arose because there was a belief that I held on to be true that was false, and it was time to replace it with the truth. And I took my focus off the Source that fueled my dreams, visions, and ideas. Awakening to my peace within fueled the journey of my unfolding consciousness. Once I returned my focus to where it was supposed to be, I was able to experience unlimited joy and most importantly, recognize my awareness as peace. I also got the courage to remove myself from the situation that placed me in the illusion and to begin to create the atmosphere of love, joy, and peace that I rightfully deserve.

TAKE THE FOCUS OFF THE ILLUSION

Here is a nugget that I would like for you to chew on: Placing your attention and intention on your greatness is the one-way ticket to peace. No matter how an illusion of a problem may occur, you have the power to shift the focus off it. I started to see that I have the power to turn any situation into a productive and peaceful one. No matter what the situation or illusion of a problem may look like, it is and can be all good. Illusion means, "something that deceives by producing a false or misleading impression of reality; the state or condition of being deceived; misapprehension." Problem means, "any question or matter involving doubt, uncertainty, or difficulty; a question proposed for solution or discussion." The definition of both words would be something like, "being deceived by a false or misleading impression of reality; being revealed as a question or matter involving doubt, uncertainty or difficulty." The illusion of a problem takes you away from knowing the true Self and the greatness that's to be expressed.

I can remember when my father and I would fix cars together. My father would tell me what his father taught him as a child, and I was elated to have this wisdom passed to me. One winter day, we were working on the rear brakes of a 1993 Ford Escort in the garage. We got stuck on how to replace the springs on the brake pads. The springs would not budge and would just snap back. At times, they even broke apart. This infuriated my father because he felt that it should be an open and close situation. In that moment, his attention wasn't on having the answer. He would get up after being extremely upset and go inside the house, leaving me alone in the cold garage. After a few minutes, my father would come back out and apologize for being upset. Then he would return to the brakes and put the spring in place without any extra effort. He would tell me that he was frustrated and couldn't understand why the springs weren't working like they should. He eventually realized that he had to give his attention to the answer to connect the springs to the brake pad. Once he was at peace, he was able to find a way to get the rusted spring back in place. This is true of a lot of situations we are confronted with. When a task doesn't turn out as easily and effortlessly as we would want, our charge is to remain calm. When we remain calm, we open ourselves to exciting ways to solve the problem.

The illusion has nothing to do with what True Essence has in store for you. It's only there to learn from; it only makes us stronger. True Essence is always giving direction and it may not seem the most popular thing to do initially. I know I would do a disservice to myself if I didn't listen. The longer I give that attention to something other than joy and peace, the longer I will be kept from joy and peace.

Something else to pay attention to is ensuring you don't make the illusion bigger than what it really is. If we allow ourselves to listen in the beginning, we can be proactive instead of reactive. I was really productive at being reactive to the illusions, by throwing a literal temper tantrum, to the point where nothing go solved because no one wanted to listen to a grown man have a tantrum. This was a form of my pain showing up and taking over, where being peace is the answer and would allow me to be open to the answer that I believed was an impossible situation. A lot of times I have noticed that the answer is always there, I just had to stay calm long enough to see it. I've had moments when my thoughts were scattered, which turned into big roadblocks, and they took me off track for the moment. I had to make a conscious decision to look for the more productive way in everything and to give my attention to the things that brought joy to my life. By doing so, I opened the door to being peace. I had to find the productive way in everything that was going on around me. Even when it seemed like it was going to hell in a hand basket, I placed my focus on being productive.

WHAT'S YOUR WHY?

I OFTEN HEARD THAT YOUR WHY HAS TO BE SO BIG that it will get you out of bed in the morning. It has to be so huge that you won't allow anything or anyone to get in the way of it manifesting. At one point in my life, I didn't understand what my WHY was and why it was so important. I figured if I just knew what I wanted to do that my WHY wouldn't be that important. I couldn't be more wrong.

Thankfully, I began to understand why my WHY was so important. Once, I worked as a customer service representative. I knew exactly what I had to do to be the best. I knew the right phrases and tone of voice to use, and I even knew how to get people to agree with me even when I was wrong. Even though I knew what to do, I took on an attitude that was less than gratitude. I wasn't happy with where I was at in life and decided to fly under the radar. I suspected that if I didn't give 100 percent, they wouldn't care or notice or expect more from me. This attitude affected my work. Even the supervisor would tell me, "I know you could do better than this, I've seen it." And you know what? She was right; I could do better than what I was doing.

One day, I watched a video by Michael Jr. – a comedian and purpose speaker – and in it, he talked about the importance of knowing your WHY. "When you know your WHY, you have options on what you can be. It has more impact because you're walking in or towards your purpose." I heard that I needed to have a WHY before, yet something about the way he said it resonated with me. I then said aloud, "Jason, now is the time to have your WHY!" That mindset couldn't have come at a better time, because I could have missed out on many blessings. At that time, my WHY was to continue to pay for the necessary lessons and programs that would build my music career, to fund my motivational speaking platform, to create my website www.jasonabenefield.com, and finish The Essential Peace of Life project. I had some things that I needed to accomplish. I had to make sure I was being a blessing to those who'd be willing to be blessed by me.

I received another confirmation when I read *The Five Ways to Success* by Nick Cannon, entertainer, music artist, and business owner. Nick shared that he worked as a mechanic and used the money he made for studio time and to help him move to Hollywood. He didn't like doing what he was doing, yet he stayed long enough to do what he needed to do to get what he wanted. And the rest is history! Even though I knew that I was greater than where I was, I had to create a better and stronger mindset. This new mindset was going to keep me focused on what I was supposed to manifest in my life.

I took my focus off the illusion of a problem and focused on my WHY. I had something bigger going on in my life, something that far surpassed the trivial fleeting experiences I had. Once I realized that it all was preparation, the process to working towards my WHY was easier and clearer. My work became the type of work that I was proud of. I felt better about myself because I was at peace. I know that there will be trials and illusions as I continue to walk my path. The difference is that now I see them as grounds for knowing and returning to my WHY.

FORGIVENESS AND GET YOUR POWER BACK

I REALIZED THAT ANOTHER THING THAT KEPT ME FROM peace was my inability to forgive. I was holding everyone and everything captive, myself included. I mastered the art of not letting go. I didn't let go of the events that harbored unproductive feelings and the people involved. Consequently, the thoughts of the illusions played like a movie in my mind. I remained upset and wanted vengeance. These feelings continued to fester because I hadn't surrendered to the peace within. I was hurting myself and felt sick.

The way out of this emotional and psychological trap was forgiveness. What does it mean to forgive? To forgive is "to renounce anger or resentment against; to excuse for a fault or an offense." I want to emphasize that when I began to forgive it wasn't for anything or anyone else, it was for me. I had given my power away by allowing what happened to boil and fester. No matter what I thought, I couldn't change the other person involved. I remember trying that when I wanted my mother to care about what was going on with me while I was dealing with the pain and trauma of seizures. The other person has their own mind set and it would only change if they changed it. All I could do was focus on me.

I bring up this topic of forgiveness because this was another process that I had to undergo to reach an awareness of peace (and it deals with the situation that I mentioned in the beginning of the chapter that had me on pins and needles). Not only did I have to calm myself down, yet I also had to surrender a higher understanding of what was happening. I had to look at the illusion and its origin. I forgave where the illusion started, and I forgave myself for giving into the illusion. I forgave myself for allowing myself to change my point of view about my life and who I am. That's forgiveness in its simplest form.

Think about it: Have you truly forgiven a person even after saying "I forgive you"? Have you walked away and never brought up the issue again to anyone? Has the person come back into your presence, and you treated them as if you're still upset? When you think about what took place, do you dwell on it for hours with negative thoughts and reenactments? Or are you finally at the place of moving on without disturbing your inner peace and the situation no longer has a hold on you? If you answered *No* to any of the preceding questions, then you haven't forgiven the person or the situation at all. If you're still holding on to the situation, I encourage you to release that person or issue because once you do, you release and free yourself.

The purpose of forgiveness is to take your attention off any issue or illusion of the problem and place your focus back on that which brings you joy. I had to realize that moving forward is the best thing for my personal health, wellbeing, and financial presence. Maintaining positive thoughts and beliefs will allow you to stay upbeat and motivated to carry on. Life is wonderful and that must be shown every day in every expression of your life. I know that if I didn't stay focused on my success, I wouldn't move on the ideas that wanted to be expressed. I wouldn't be on the same page as Source, and I'd be unproductive. Negative thoughts and beliefs would have acquired the space where greatness should be. The goal is to remove the distractions that would hinder movement and growth and anything that would block what True Essence has prepared for you.

It's so powerful to say, "I forgive me!" There is nothing you can do that will change what happened; however, you can learn from it. When you forgive yourself, you are giving yourself permission to be free from something that kept you bound to the past. The goal here is peace and to get peace, you must be diligent in releasing anything that holds you down and back from your greatness.

GIVING THANKS

1 Thessalonians 5:18 of the Bible says, "In everything give thanks for this is the will of God concerning you." Giving thanks is a form of being peace. When I began to say, "Thank You," I was expressing gratitude, appreciation, and acknowledgement. I had the ability to change my current circumstance into something that would bring joy into my life. I didn't have to stay where I was, and my mindset didn't have to be a permanent one. Being grateful allows me to focus on what is mine to achieve – my dreams, visions, and ideas. Being grateful kept me from allowing worry to overtake the greatness that was happening.

Many times, I would wake up in the middle of the

night and begin to think about things that would rattle my peaceful mood. I would concentrate on my bank account, the type of job that I had, and the bills that had to be paid. All of this would take precedence over the fact that I was already successful and able to complete the tasks at hand. I took a different route and began to say, "Thank You." As I did, it assuaged the internal fight in my mind.

I encourage you to begin being thankful for everyday things, like being alive. Be thankful for the ability to get up, move, and eat on your own. Be thankful for the ability to pay your bills and maintain the roof over your head. Be thankful for the truth that everything is working for your good. Begin to give thanks and as you do, do something that brings you joy.

BEING PEACE

Being Peace allows you to have a clear mind. Being peace opens you to being productive with that is to express in your life. Being Peace also allows you to retain information better. I noticed that as I allowed peace to express, I could pay attention to details that I'd otherwise forget or overlook. I stayed focused on the task at hand and learned new and exciting things. I realized the power I had in being peace and how much I could do through peace.

I would like you to feel the joy! Being peace is feeling joy and the assurance that all is well with you right now. Everything is working together for your productivity. When you are feeling the joy, you smile at life. Once I made the decision to overcome a thought or situation that tried to hold me back, I realized I had already won. I'm not letting the illusion of problems get in my way of feeling joy and I hope you do the same. There is a quote by Zig Ziglar that is appropriate here and it says, "It's not what happens to you that determines how far you will go in life; it is how you handle what happens to you." When someone tells you, "No" in their house, find a way for "yes" to be the answer in your house. Every ending isn't an ending. It's an opportunity for a new beginning to emerge and a greater opportunity to be peace.

WRAPPING UP

I want to encourage you to get excited about whatever you put your mind to. Get even more excited for the endless possibilities that await you once you realize what is available for you to co-create. Living in your productiveness is contagious, and the people around you will want the same for themselves. They will begin to speak about the ideas they have and will find ways to attain the knowledge to create them. When you allow yourself to be peace, it ignites and inspires others to do the same.

If you ever find yourself in a space of doubt, I invite you to imagine me saying to you, "You can do it. You have the power. Only you can unfold into a better you!" There will be people who can assist you in the process of fulfilling your visions, yet it is up to you to finish the work. It is up to you to move toward your rightful inheritance, which has already been prepared for you. Take the necessary steps and open your mind to the peace that is essential for life.

BIBLIOGRAPHY

Addington, Jack & Cornelia, *The Perfect Power Within You* (Marina Del Rey, CA: DeVorss & Company 1973)

Addington, Jack Ensign, *Psychogenesis: Everything Begins in Mind* (Marina Del Rey, CA: DeVorss & Company, 1971)

Amplified Version of the Bible

Beckwith, Michael Bernard, *The Life Visioning Process* (Louisville, CO: Sounds True, 2008)

"Dhammapada" *Dhammapada (English Translation)*. 2003. 12 Dec. 2012 http://myweb.ncku.edu.tw/~Isn46/Tipitaka/Sutta/khuddaka/Dhammapada/Dhp.English.htm.

Fox, Emmet, *Mental Equivalent* (Unity Village, MO: Unity, 1943)

Hill, Napoleon, *Golden Rules* (New York: Wiley Publishing, 2008)

King James Version of the Bible

Maxwell, John C., *Developing the Leader Within You* (Nashville, TN: Thomas Nelson Inc.1993)

Munroe, Dr. Myles, *The Spirit of Leadership* (New Kensington, PA: Whitaker House, 2005)

Nightingale, Earl, *The Strangest Secret* (Wheeling, IL: Nightingale-Conant Corporation, 1986)

Russell, Robert, *Making the Contact* (Marina Del Rey, CA: DeVorss & Company, 1956)

Shakespeare, William, *Hamlet* (New York: Simon & Schuster, 2003)

Williamson, Marianne, *A Return to Love* (New York: HarperCollins Publisher, 1996)

Ziegler, Meseena, "How One Woman Went from Homeless to Millionaire in Less Than Two Years" Forbes.com, Forbes Magazine, 15 Feb. 2013 <http://shine.yahoo.com/secrets-to-your-

Bibliography

success/one-woman-went-homeless-millionaire-less-two-years-19220035.html>

www.ingramcontent.com/pod-product-compliance
Lightning Source LLC
Chambersburg PA
CBHW060103230426
43661CB00033B/1406/J